THE H...
BOOK...
MANAGE...

THE HONDA BOOK OF MANAGEMENT

A LEADERSHIP PHILOSOPHY FOR HIGH INDUSTRIAL SUCCESS

SETSUO MITO

KOGAN PAGE

First published in Japan in 1980 by Diamond/Sha Company
of Tokyo as *The Honda Management System: Japanese Management
Practice*

First published in Great Britain in 1990
by The Athlone Press Ltd
1 Park Drive, London NW11 7SG
and 171 First Avenue, Atlantic Highlands, NJ 07716

This edition first published in Great Britain in 1990 by
Kogan Page Ltd
120 Pentonville Road, London N1 9JN

British Library Cataloguing in Publication Data

A CIP record for this book is available from the British Library.

ISBN 0–7494–0201–6

Typeset by J&L Composition Ltd, Filey, North Yorkshire
Printed and bound in Great Britain by
Biddles Ltd, Guildford and Kings Lynn

Contents

Preface

The preparation of the manuscript for this book began in 1983. Since that time, the text has gone through many transformations – the greatest being translation into English – before the book was finally printed. The Honda Motor Company has, of course, continued growing and maturing over these years. The management system I have described in detail here represents the enduring, strong, and resilient trunk of the Honda tree, and its role in maintaining the corporation's dynamism is as vigorous as ever.

Tadashi Kume, the president of Honda since 1983, is the third head of the company. He and his colleagues have maintained the spirit of entrepreneurship of the founders Sōichiro Honda and Takeo Fujisawa; they have nourished the organizational framework of the company, and devoted themselves to group conceptualization and system management. They have cultivated an approach that is both creative and destructive – in other words, it both creates systems and destroys them, whichever is in the best interests of the company.

Hondaism and the Honda management system possess, I believe, a universality that transcends any single corporation, industry, or even country. The company's success when it moved into direct investment in the United States, Europe, and Southeast Asia bears out this belief. For this reason, this book concentrates particularly on the way the Honda management system came into being and how it works.

And while I believe in the universality of Honda management, it is also part of the often-baffling Japanese way of doing business. It is not easy to explain, and was doubly so for the translators, who had to read between the lines, ferret out the unspoken assumptions, and straighten out the distortions resulting from the narrow perspective of a Japanese author. I would like to thank the staff of the Center for Social Science Communication for overcoming these obstacles and creating a logical, lucid English version. Both the translators and myself are also extremely grateful for the efforts of the editors at The Athlone Press.

Finally, I wish to express my profound appreciation to the many people at Honda Motors Co. for providing me with useful, reliable data and complying with my numerous requests for interviews.

Setsuo Mito
September 1989

Foreword

This translation of Setsuo Mito's account of the management system in the Honda Motor Company (HMC) provides a unique opportunity for the non-Japanese reader to gain a deeper insight into the nature of managerial roles in Japan. Although the Honda case has a number of special characteristics, it can be viewed as an example of one of a number of outstandingly successful Japanese manufacturing companies which have risen to prominence in the international scene since the Second World War. Such companies have clearly been driven by highly expert decision-takers and it is pertinent to ask *how* such expertise has been developed and *what* it actually amounts to. Existing studies of HMC in English have emphasised the character of Sōichirō Honda, the founder of the company (Sakiya 1982, Sanders 1975) and his impact on the products developed and marketed. What needs to be discussed is the part played by the management system built up by Mr Honda and his associates and the light this throws on the concepts and assumptions of the managerial role in Japan.

GENERAL CONCEPTS OF JAPANESE MANAGEMENT

The topic of 'Japanese Management' has appeared regularly in recent years in discussions at management conferences and is usually contrasted with the traditional assumptions of 'American Management' (Ouchi 1981, Pascale, & Athos 1980). The main ideas associated with 'Japanese Management' in the West are often poorly defined but are essentially an argument for equality as a basis for competition and co-operation. There are seven crucial ideas which summarise the approach:

1. All members of an organisation should feel collective responsibility for the success of that organisation.
2. All employees should be flexible enough to perform a wide variety of roles; they need to be trained to allow them to do this effectively.
3. Subordinates need to be trusted to get on with their work; they have potential which has to be developed.
4. All employees need to be protected whilst working for the organisation so that they can give their maximum effort to solving work problems.
5. Employees need to have a life career within the organisation to stimulate their loyalty and motivation to develop their skills and innate capacities.
6. Management must be governed by a philosophy of 'pragmatic rationalism' to allow changes in new circumstances.
7. Management must pursue a philosophy of the 'michi', the 'way' which underlines the importance of daily interaction with work colleagues and a shared identity with them in solving work problems.

THE HONDA APPROACH TO MANAGEMENT

Mito's account of Honda management principles can be placed squarely within this general approach. There is no conflict with these seven statements, but, at the same time, he makes it clear that the company has developed a very special approach which distinguishes it from many other Japanese companies. The book concentrates on the *leadership philosophy* and how this permeates four crucial aspects of managerial and organisational behaviour. This can be shown diagramatically:

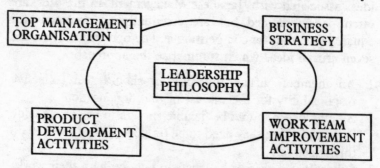

It is important to stress the key role played by the *leadership philosophy* in setting guidelines for the personal behaviour of employees at every level. This is the reality of neo-Confucian thinking; management has the duty to lay down a clear normative framework for all work activities. As Ronald Dore emphasises, a 'Confucian' approach means a design for economic institutions that 'brings out the best in people' (Dore 1987). Such an approach inevitably means articulating a coherent managerial ideology. There are many examples given by Mito. 'Simultaneous competition among different approaches', 'self-reliance', and the 'complementarity principle' are all normative and ideological statements.

Many Western readers react to such statements by suspecting that managerial intentions are not the same as actual employee actions. Why should employees share such beliefs when their interests are often directly opposed to managerial plans and objectives? Surely Japan is no different from other countries in the realities of industrial relations?

What needs to be emphasised here is that Japanese management depends on the belief that conscious articulation of normative slogans is necessary to guide employee behaviour; even if such slogans meet apathetic or direct resistance. That judgement rests on a history of hundreds of years of moral leadership adopted by the ruling elite in society. The success of Japanese enterprises since World War II seems to show some evidence that the approach still achieves results in modern Japanese society. It is, of course, relevant to question whether this will continue to be the case in the medium and long-term future.

THE HONDA LEADERSHIP PHILOSOPHY

There are some strikingly different emphases in the Honda leadership philosophy compared with more traditional companies. 'Individualism' is *not* seen as anti-social; individual competition and group competition is sponsored and there is an enormous emphasis on originality and freedom for individuals to express their own ideas and ways of approaching work problems. Honda is clearly opposed to conformity and bureaucratic order. The demands of change are seen as making continuous shifts in ideas necessary.

A careful reading of the text, however, should prevent readers jumping to the conclusion that Honda is advocating a 'California style' work organisation based only on individual rationality. Individualism is seen as crucial *within* the assumption of collective loyalty and co-operation. Freedom of expression is *within* the acceptance of the overall goals of the organisation. What is advocated is a climate of freedom and creativity, but this does not rule out social relations or collective goals. This attempted synthesis of individualism and collectivism is one of the more striking characteristics of the Honda approach.

TOP MANAGEMENT ORGANISATION

Mito describes at some length how the institution of the 'Joint Boardroom' was created and how it apparently works. Basically, the concept is that of project management applied to top management (Board of Directors) positions. The physical construction of an open-plan office for Directors emphasises their daily working relations on jointly-owned problems, rather than the symbolism of the boardroom table and council room which speaks only of joint discussions and joint decisions in periodic meetings. The team management role of Directors is thus more important than their hierarchical position or access for exercising 'political' influence.

How should such a radical idea be evaluated? Is Honda really so egalitarian? Are Directors devalued by such an institution?

In the context of Japanese capitalism, the idea of a 'working director' is neither strange nor unduly radical. The terminology used by the translators – President, Vice-Presidents, Executive Directors, Directors, etc – is misleading if these titles are taken to mean distinct jobs and positions on an organisation chart. Nearly all Japanese firms distinguish 'status position' attached to the person of individual managers, according to his seniority and personally recognised capacity, from the actual work roles and tasks assigned to such managers. The latter vary with circumstances and do not affect the former. Status order is often very important and this is symbolised by the seating position at desks within an open office. The Honda 'Joint Boardroom' is no exception to this and status can be distinguished within the Director team.

It is also true that most Directors, or Board members, in Japanese firms are simply senior managers who have come up the hierarchy in their life career. Honda has a record of younger Managing Directors and does not emphasise the use of Director roles as a place for senior managers who have officially retired from the normal management hierarchy, i.e. after the age of 55, as found in many traditionally orientated companies. Nevertheless the Honda system of Directors is within the general Japanese approach of 'working director'. Probably the most original feature of the Honda system is the deployment of Directors in teams to develop strategic responses to major issues.

BUSINESS STRATEGY

There are a number of examples given in the book of major shifts in Honda's policy objectives, given the development of changes in the market situation or the political/economic environment facing the firm. None of these are surprising in themselves; what is remarkable is the willingness to shift product development or market strategies so radically and so quickly. The internationalisation strategy is an excellent example of this. Many Japanese firms have followed the logic of Honda, very few did it so quickly and with such confidence. Very few have moved so quickly from relatively simple products to more complex ones or have mastered the changes in the types of technology required so successfully. All this reflects a high degree of integration in planning between sales, engineering development and production and extremely effective horizontal communications.

The Honda story tends in this book, as in others, to be presented as a heroic tale of the company versus the world. This is clearly the way that it is presented inside the company. Making allowances for this, however, it has to be said that Honda is an excellent example of a company which uses aggressive and dramatic strategies. It has suffered a number of set-backs as a result of this type of risk-taking, but the capacity to learn from mistakes clearly is considerable. All this must have an organisational basis and implies a climate in which learning is encouraged.

PRODUCT DEVELOPMENT ACTIVITIES

The core of the business strategies adopted is described by Mito as the matching of market opportunities with newly developed products. The development process is thus at the heart of the company's activities. This judgement is common among most Japanese manufacturing firms. The sponsoring of talent among engineers and scientists is crucial to an effective development process. How has this been achieved?

Mito is fairly explicit about the policies used for sponsoring an effective development process and they are probably the most important arguments in the book, seen from the viewpoint of foreign readers.

Firstly, development is placed in a situation where there is a long-term and emotive objective, similar to that of Kennedy in the Moon Apollo programme. Development has to be aimed at an exciting and important achievement, which will be seen by the world at large as significant and right. Technical and scientific work has to be focused on really important possibilities.

Second, any idea which might help to solve the problems involved should be tried, no matter how unconventional. Individuals who think that they might have a better solution to that favoured by the majority, should be given finance and support to try out their ideas. Individual researchers can be asked to compete with each other in finding the best solution.

Thirdly, technical management should support their project teams throughout their trials and successes; even when they fail they should go on supporting them. This motivates technical staff not to give up.

Fourthly, there has to be a specific institutional formal mechanism for selecting the most promising research projects for actual development. This is the role of the Development Evaluation Committee. It is comprised of representatives of sales, engineering, personnel management and international affairs among other functional departments. This means that development decisions are never taken purely from a technical perspective.

Such policies can be found in other major Japanese corporations but the Honda emphasis on sponsoring original solutions is relatively unique. Technical excellence is clearly a major goal and this leads to rapid product development.

WORKTEAM IMPROVEMENT ACTIVITIES

As in other Japanese firms, Honda, according to Mito, places a lot of emphasis on worker circle activity in trying to improve the quality of product and process, reduce costs, improve safety and quality of work life conditions, etc. Honda Sōichirō is quoted as telling his employees not to work for the company, but for their own satisfaction. 'Every human being has the desire to improve' argued Honda and this desire has to be stimulated. The circle activity is logical to such a philosophy.

THE SIGNIFICANCE OF THE BOOK

Honda is not the only successful manufacturer of motor cars in Japan and would certainly not be seen in Japan as a 'typical' firm. It is clearly dangerous therefore to generalise from this case too much about 'Japanese' experience.

Mr Mito's book is also necessarily selective in its coverage of HMC. In a text of this length, there can be no full treatment of industrial relations or personnel policy; nor a full discussion of joint-venture relationship with foreign firms such as Rover; nor room to discuss the competitive position of Honda within Japan and its struggle with Toyota and Nissan. The policies of its enterprise union – which is highly independent of union federations – are not discussed, nor the contrast with the struggle with the American UAW organisation.

The book's significance lies in the insight provided into the relationship between ideas and behaviour in the Japanese context. There are many examples of the unconventional style of Mr Sōichirō Honda; of how he used shock tactics to create dreams and ideas of possible innovations. Although the man himself was clearly a remarkable individual, none of the achievements of the company would have been possible without the development of a special managerial approach.

The approach was itself innovative and readers can savour the taste for themselves.

Keith Thurley
London School of Economics
University of London

References

Dore, R P (1987) *Taking Japan Seriously: A Confucian Perspective on Leading Economic issues*, The Athlone Press, London.

Ouchi, W (1981) *Theory Z; How American Business can meet the Japanese Challenge*, Addison and Wesley.

Pascale, R T & A G Athos (1981) *The Art of Japanese Management: Applications for American Executives*, Simon and Schuster, New York.

Sakiya, T (1982) *Honda Motor; the Men, the Management, the Machines*, Kodansha International, Tokyo.

Sanders, S (1975) *Honda, the Man and his Machines*, Little, Brown, Boston.

1

The Spirit of Hondaism

INDIVIDUALISM AND SELF-RELIANCE

In its own words, the Honda Motor Company (HMC) seeks to
'make reasonably priced and superior products to meet our
customers' needs', and this is set 'in a global perspective'.
However, if we ask those who work at Honda what the
philosophy of the enterprise is – what Hondaism means to
them – we get different answers, but this is in accord with the
spirit of Hondaism which is not a fixed set of rules. In
practice, Hondaism requires its employees to do a conscientious
job. It calls upon them to use their imagination, to set up their
own code of behaviour and decide on their own goals. Freedom
and respect for the individual are at the heart of the matter:
they are the ideals shared by all Honda personnel – young and
old, executive and line worker alike – and they are part and
parcel of the company's tradition and corporate culture.

Despite the rich diversity of personalities in Honda and the
many interpretations of Hondaism, there is a shared vocabulary.
Never forgotten are the personal mottoes of the founders,
Sōichirō Honda (b.1906) and Takeo Fujisawa (b.1910):

> Be original.
> Do not rely on government.
> Work for your own sake.

All three rules are fundamental in Hondaism but perhaps the first – Be original – takes pride of place. Sōichirō Honda's regard for originality goes back to the pre-war days when he ran a small workshop in Hamamatsu in Shizuoka prefecture. Fascinated with the latest aircraft, cars and motorcycles which were then being made in the United States and Europe, he saw how Japanese technology was behind the times. The gap was immense and could not be closed overnight. But Honda believed that Japan could catch up – not through imitation (as was the general practice at the time) – but by developing its own technology. Even in his crude local workshop he spoke of the need to develop technology in 'a global perspective'.

He recalls that after the war, when motorcycle racing first took place in Japan, there were young men in the company who loved racing above all else. When they began racing, he helped them a lot even though they usually lost. At that time there were several motorcycle manufacturers in Japan but they made engines that were mere copies of the leading foreign makes such as Triumph and Adler.

At first Honda's motorcycles came nowhere near their rivals, but Honda could not bear the thought of simply imitating foreign models: no matter what, he was determined to come up with a better, original machine of his own. It took a long time and a great deal of effort but the company eventually caught up with its rivals, and later overtook them. The companies that had prospered by imitating did well at first, but lost out later on. Honda saw what happens when imitation becomes habitual and the problems that such a policy poses for the integrity and health of a company. To put short-term results before creative, original effort, he said, was to court ultimate downfall.

Honda understood the temptations of taking the easy way but mere copying gives the technician no pride of creation. The notion of creativity in Japan has always been a little ambiguous. Catch-phrases such as 'creativity begins with imitation' and 'imitation is part of creation' are often used to cover up a lack of originality. Honda and his protégés were especially careful to make the distinction between creating and copying, and to avoid the pitfalls of imitation.

Here, self-reliance – Do not rely on government – comes into the picture. From the time of its incorporation in 1948 to the present day, Honda management has never sought official aid or protection. Even during hard times, the company did not ask for government help – a common enough practice among businesses in Japan – but got out of difficulties on its own. Honda also accepted competition by foreign products and capital. It is one of the few companies that has consistently urged greater market access for goods, services and capital. Nor has Honda adopted the practice found in many large companies of appointing retired bureaucrats to advisory or top management positions in order to try and secure influence with government.

Honda's management principles and practices, based on free competition and self-reliance, embody the true spirit of entrepreneurship. Though its approach is not revolutionary, the Honda Company was once looked upon as a maverick in Japanese industrial circles where a premium was placed on solidarity and acting in unison. Honda's consistent belief was that manufacturers could never be internationally competitive if they relied on government to try and ensure their survival. While there is a tendency in Japanese industry to voice lofty principles while paying them only lip service, Honda has got on with setting goals and taking steps to reach them. Today, with the internationalisation of Japan's economy, the merits of Honda's style of management are being recognised.

Another key element of Hondaism is 'work for your own sake', an expression of the company's action-orientated approach. The willingness to be self-effacing and to commit oneself to the group has a tradition in Japan. But today there is little to be achieved by actions motivated purely 'for the sake of the country' or 'for the sake of the company'. 'To work for your own sake' is what comes naturally to most people and underlies Honda's management philosophy.

CONTROL AND ORGANISATION

In the early years, Sōichirō Honda and Takeo Fujisawa carried the company along with their own forceful personal leadership. Part of their genius was to manage without organisational charts and diagrams: they exercised control intuitively. In October 1973, they both retired, recognising that the company had grown to a size that called for an explicit organisational scheme. They had the confidence to leave the company in the hands of younger leaders whose thinking was flexible and creative and who could turn corporate goals into real accomplishments.

Before retiring, Honda and Fujisawa saw to it that the organisational scheme of the corporation was clearly set out. Fujisawa had anticipated this need with his original idea for a 'joint boardroom'. This arrangement became the centrepiece for a management strategy aimed at the global market. With the implementation of the system in 1964, top management literally gathered together in the same room where they discussed and examined fundamental questions such as What is a corporation? What is management? What are the duties of company executives?

The joint boardroom is one of the means through which company leadership implements the principles of Hondaism. The joint boardroom was set up and then set aside time and time again, both as a concept and as a physical arrangement, before it finally became institutionalised as a way of planning and decision-making. Executives with particular roles and responsibilities present their own points of view, and out of this process measures are taken to achieve given goals or to create new objectives.

It was Kiyoshi Kawashima (b.1928), currently director and

top adviser, who took a leading role in defining Hondaism while he was company president during 1973–83. Before then, he had been president (1971–73) of Honda Research and Development.

COMPETITIVE TEAM WORK

Honda R & D, now a wholly-owned subsidiary of HMC, became independent in July 1960. It was set up for the purpose of 'brain-storming' and technological development; it was staffed with people of enterprise and with the ability to innovate. It grew vigorously through staff teamwork and the direct input of the founder who knew how to tap the potential of each researcher – by fatherly encouragement, or by playing devil's advocate or by sheer benevolence. Honda R & D is a fine example of Sōichirō genius and style.

Entrepreneurship and the spirit of innovation are both basic ingredients of Hondaism. Kiyoshi Kawashima and Tadashi Kume (b.1932 and HMC president in 1983) both served as presidents of Honda R & D before rising to the top position in the parent company, an experience that gave them a proper understanding of Honda's ideals. Under Kawashima, the basic philosophy of Hondaism was made explicit and the role and responsibilities of Honda R & D as a HMC subsidiary made crystal clear. In large part, it was to 'supply the Honda Motor Company of which R & D are an inseparable part, with product designs based on advanced research in a wide variety of fields through the free application of the individual abilities and talents of its staff.'

Once Honda became a large corporation, its managers had to have an organisational scheme upon which to run the business, but even more important they had to be able to translate the ideals of the enterprise into easily understandable language. Once people understood what was going on, they could better communicate with one another. When Kawashima became president of HMC, the in-house jargon he had developed during his years as head of Honda R & D began to spread to all the companies in the Honda group and was elevated to the level of a company cult and a management system.

'Simultaneous competition among different approaches' – also called 'individual play and team strategy' – (as described later on in chapter 3) is part of that jargon. It aptly described the philosophy and practice not only of Honda R & D but the entire Honda group. It means discovering the special abilities of each researcher and harnessing them for creative endeavour. It means providing the conditions for both individuals and teams to work effectively in generating new ideas within the limited time they have in the competitive world: it means finding people's true calling through the shared experience of pursuing original research and all its joys and hardships.

'Simultaneous competition among different approaches' is both a slogan of the group and a tool of daily practice. Every person is unique and any given objective can be reached in different ways. Individuals will choose different ways and Honda lets them do so – guiding them onwards but leaving them to explore problems in their own way and in competition with each other. Because of the premium on time, management must keep tabs on the projects under way, giving signals – stop, go, speed up, slow down – so that research efforts converge at the final goal. The relationship between researchers (whose freedom to engage in creative thought must be respected) and the managers (whose signals must help to get the work done in good time) is one both of co-operation and conflict. To make this relationship work, the two sides must have a clear picture of their responsibilities to one another.

The 'simultaneous competition among different approaches' technique is a key part of the set of ideas that governs the Honda organisation today. Through it, many products of quite remarkable originality came into being: the Road Pal motorcycle, the Tact scooter, the Dream CB line of motorcycles as well as the

Civic, Accord and City cars. Each is the product of the kind of competition that is fostered among Honda's research staff.

INSTRUCTION AND EXAMPLE

The company mottoes sum up the philosophy of Honda's founder, and these are supplemented by five golden rules:

1. Follow your dreams and keep a youthful outlook.
2. Respect theory, new ideas, and time.
3. Love your work and make your workplace bright and positive.
4. Ensure a smooth flow of work.
5. Make research and dedicated effort a daily habit.

These are simple and familiar statements, but *acting* on them is not easy. When brought within the fabric of Hondaism, they can be made to work and Honda employees take them very seriously.

The key words and fundamental elements of the five rules are 'dreams', 'youthful', 'theory', 'ideas', 'time', 'love of work', 'a bright and positive workplace', 'harmony', 'the flow of work', 'research', and 'effort'. All are basic elements both of individual and organisational activities. In every activity they are the objectives, the yardsticks of achievement and the guide to co-ordinated and improved thinking.

None of these ideals, however, would be achieved without the practical know-how of able leaders. The organisation's head must be able to translate ideals into reality and undertake constant self-appraisal. Kiyoshi Kawashima was fanatical about putting the company's mottoes and the five principles into practice; he believed that once they were firmly established, the organisation would develop still further. He had a check-list of criteria against which management practices were contantly appraised such as:

Are we giving the staff the chance to use their imagination?
Is there enough youthfulness and courage in the leadership
to prevent the organisation from becoming bureaucratic?
Are we giving proper attention to developing theory and
putting theory into practice?
Are we being sufficiently receptive to the free flow of new
ideas?
Are our decisions made at the right time?

The typical presidents of big businesses in Japan lead rather
a coddled life, conserving their energy and watching their
health with great care so as to remain in power as long as
possible. Very few ever admit it when they become worn out
by their responsibilities nor will they willingly pass on their
position to younger leaders.

Kawashima became president at the age of 45. When he
retired at 55, he said, 'I have burned all the energy I had to
give during these ten years as president. I now need time off to
recharge and refuel. In any case, a change of leadership is vital
in order to keep the organisation young and vigorous'. Like
his mentors, Honda and Fujisawa, he retired gracefully and
decisively. Knowing when to finish is important in any
endeavour, and the timely change-over of the presidency of
Honda helped to secure the ideals of Hondaism even more
firmly than ever.

DECISION-MAKING

The speed and efficiency of decision-making among Honda's
top management are often remarked upon. It was the first in
the industry to build a plant in the United States, setting up a
motorcycle plant in Ohio in 1978, and later constructing a car
plant in the same State. This helped not only to placate the
strong protectionist movement in the United States but also to
ease economic friction between the two countries.

By now all the major carmakers in Japan have undertaken

(or have plans to undertake) direct investment projects in the United States but Honda was the first in the field, and the others did not carry out their plans until well into the 1980s. Toyota's factory, jointly run by General Motors in Freemont, California, did not begin operations until the end of 1984. Production of cars at Nissan's Tennessee plant started in March 1985 (knock-down production of trucks had begun earlier). Mazda's plan was to construct a plant in Michigan in 1987. Mitsubishi decided to start operations in the United States in 1988.

Why was Honda so quick to decide on this type of project and to carry it through? The nature of the company and the way it is managed gave it a head start. Because it has two divisions, one for two-wheeled and the other for four-wheeled vehicles, Honda enjoys more options for managerial strategies than other manufacturers. It began to think about car production in the United States as early as 1975, and after careful preparation and planning, it set the project in motion in April 1978. Its strategy was shrewd, beginning with the Ohio motorcycle plant and moving gradually towards the construction of a car plant. Other reasons why decision-making at Honda is rapid are as follows:

1. Honda makes a variety of export products including motorcycles, cars and agricultural machinery, and has long experience in knock-down production and local production in overseas plants. In November 1989 Honda exported to 150 countries and had 74 plants (including those engaged in knock-down production) in 38 countries. This experience, first in the production of two-wheeled vehicles, gave Honda's management a wealth of know-how that Toyota and Nissan could not match. The fact that many Honda employees have experience in overseas management is another source of strength.
2. Another advantage Honda enjoys is that it can begin a local project with a relatively modest investment in motorcycle

production. Launching the production of four-wheeled vehicles in a foreign country requires a huge investment in plant and equipment and is that much more risky. Honda, unlike Toyota and Nissan, could start with a motorcycle plant and build a car plant once the first project was under way.

3. Success in one local project helps in the supply of capital funds, making it possible to plough profits back into further overseas investment without outside aid. When the plant was built in Ohio, only 20 per cent of the funds came from Japan; the remaining 80 per cent came from the accumulated funds of the American Honda Motor Company (established in 1959) in the United States itself. Today the Ohio plants have a self-financing reinvestment programme.

4. Honda's investment efficiency in plant is high because close attention is given to cost and profit margins. Cost control and quality control have clearly been much tighter at Toyota and Nissan (which concentrate on products with low margins centering on small cars) than at American plants making large cars for which the profit ratio is high. This policy of Japanese carmakers is responsible for the competitive strength of their products in the small car market. At Honda, monitoring cost is especially rigorous. In the case of the popular Super Cub 50cc motorcycle, Honda ventured to reduce its profit margin to less than ¥10,000 ($42) apiece, and this made for lower costs and high investment efficiency.

5. Direct investment overseas means building plants overseas and depriving Japanese labour of the benefits they might enjoy if the plants were built in Japan. Honda's management reached an understanding with the company's labour union at an early stage, and this helped decision-making on overseas direct investment.

6. The last but perhaps the most important reason for Honda's record of rapid decision-making, is the view that what makes each person unique is a difference not of ability but

of character. Kiyoshi Kawashima made this idea a rule of management policy, emphasising its importance in working with people of other countries. Acceptance of this idea has proved of great help in dealing with problems in the international economy.

For many years Japanese carmakers were wary about building plants in the United States out of scepticism about the performance of American workers and antipathy towards American institutions such as the labour unions. Honda's acceptance of American-style labour unions and its willingness to 'do in Rome as the Romans do' was quite exceptional. It is true that environment affects individual personality and ability: thus, education can make a difference to the amount of knowledge people acquire. At first glance these variables may seem to be responsible for differences in ability. But how well people are educated or what their environment is while growing up is not the decisive factor in their work performance. Honda's approach to the problem has been to provide a stimulating environment that gets people to *want* to learn. In turn, the learning experience promotes creativity and brings out the special traits and talents of each and every person.

Honda has applied the principle of giving more emphasis to individual character than to levels of ability in each country where it has expanded. This emphasis on individuality and the 'human touch' has been built up from the company's experience in international enterprise over the years.

THE AGE OF INFORMATION

Manpower, materials, and money are the three main components of any business, but with the advance of the computer age, information is now an indispensable input. In Japan, 1985 was a turning point in the information revolution, prompting people to dub it the 'first year of the information era' and the 'beginning of the age of the New Media'. One of the significant events during the year was the privatisation of Nippon Telegraph and Telephone (NTT), formerly a public corporation, which then led in the bidding for a project to build a new information network system (INS), and NTT aims to complete a sophisticated data processing and communications system by the year 2000. This will create a firm foundation for the information-orientated society through the marriage of computers and communications technology.

The goal of the INS project is to switch the telephone network from the present analog to digital signals in order to make it compatible with other networks for telegraph, data and facsimile transmission. The merit of this system is that it will eliminate differences in telephone charges based on distance. Using new equipment such as optical fibre and communications satellites, the INS will link homes with workplaces, banks, department stores, hospitals, libraries, local government offices and public facilities. Moreover, it will make two-way communication possible using television-telephones, the CAPTAIN system (Character and Pattern Telephone Access Information Network), VRS (Video Response System) and facsimile-received newspapers.

Already there are many domestic and internationally linked information networks being built in Japan such as VAN (Value-added Network) and LAN (Local Area Network), and fierce competition between domestic as well as foreign companies has developed to capture the largest share of the market. Private corporations, too, are seeking to develop flexible and elaborate management information systems that can keep pace with developments. Honda is no exception and rapid progress has been made on its management information system. At the company's new headquarters, opened in Tokyo in August 1985, the new system is in full-scale operation.

The extent to which the Honda management system will grow through information-processing and office automation depends on how good a data base is created and how it is used.

The symbol of the information age is the computer terminal keyboard. Another is the ID card used by individual operators in various accounting systems. In great need, moreover, are systems that will permit the retrieval of necessary information. Simulation systems for co-ordinating analysis on the basis of that information for effective problem-solving are equally important.

Honda's original data base had, at the least, to contain inter-plant information on production control, accounting, quality control, domestic-made cars, motorcycles and agricultural machinery, conditions overseas, and personnel management. It had to be available on-line to all parts of the Honda group, including research and development, engineering and sales as well as to its sales agents, suppliers and other subcontractors. In addition to this in-house data base, the company also makes full use of available external data bases.

Hondaism has a unique role to play in the information society for even if highly advanced hardware is developed through technological innovation and quality software is created to make use of it, it is by and for human beings that both must be used. The attitudes and powers of the people – the 'humanware' – who control and benefit from technology must be taken into account.

The potential of the human mind is expected to be even more fully displayed in the years to come, ushering in the advanced information society in the full sense of the term. One of Honda's most important concerns is to identify and refine those aspects of business that can only be properly handled by human beings. The work falls into two main categories, 'brain work' and 'routine work'. At Honda today, the former accounts for about 56 per cent of all the work and the latter for about 44 per cent. At the time of the first oil crisis in 1973, the figures were 30 per cent and 70 per cent respectively, showing how much more important human input has become. By the 1990s, the company hopes to raise the proportion of brain-work to 80 per cent.

To that end, Honda is seeking to expand its 'experts system'. Some effort has been made to train more specialists in administration and sales but more weight has been given to cultivating personnel skills. Efforts have been made from early on in the company's history to move away from a pyramid-like organisation to one with a horizontal structure, reducing the number of managerial posts as much as possible and shortening the vertical lines of communication in order to make for a more efficient flow of information.

The new emphasis on training people in office work (dubbed the 'Ex-O' drive) is meant to create experts in the kinds of tasks only humans can perform. They will be skilled at selecting the data necessary (now or in the near future) for the 'brain work' side of company business. This is an important new statement of Hondaism.

The nature of Honda's internationalism is sure to change with the progress of the information society. Ultimately it will make no difference where in the world the decision-making of the company takes place: we can even envisage a sort of 'mobile boardroom'. The world (at least in the United States, the Western European countries, Japan and the countries of South-east Asia) is becoming closely linked through various communications systems. The exchange of information is basically free and equally shared, providing conditions that Honda can exploit to its benefit.

The opening of the new company headquarters and the advance of information and automation systems are a powerful new force behind the internationalism for which Honda is famous, namely, its localisation efforts. Honda's progress has gone through various stages – beginning with product localisation (the export of products), profit localisation (whereby profits are reinvested in the host country instead of being brought back to the parent company), and then production localisation (building plants overseas and employing local workers).

MANAGEMENT LOCALISATION

Today Honda is starting to transfer research and development as well as design (of cars and motorcycles for overseas markets) to local initiative. Products for the American market will be developed and designed by Americans, products for the Common Market by Europeans, and so on. Honda's top management believes that it is no longer necessary for headquarters or Honda R & D to control all decision-making and design activities in its overseas subsidiaries. The time has come to set up a management organisation that gives a lot of autonomy to 'Honda' corporations around the world while each corporation retains its links with the group through the unified sales, engineering and development system – the SED system.

Setting up Honda Research of America in California in September 1984 and Honda Research of Europe in West Germany in January 1985 were the first steps towards this goal. Both are research and development bodies that merged existing sales and production activities, thus completing the SED triad in the United States and Europe. With these systems in operation, Honda's unique approach and strategies are put into effect in these two regions, making it possible to develop highly competitive new car and motorcycle models at local levels.

The localisation of Honda's management effectively decentralises decision-making powers; not that this will weaken the management structure or fragment the organisation. For example, the trilateral Japan–US–Europe relationship will enjoy a shared experience. If a new car developed by Honda of America turns out to have a wider appeal, the design or the finished product can be offered to partners in Japan and Europe, and vice versa. Thus the success of a new product developed in one region can be shared by others.

Honda foresees that the top management of these partner

corporations will confer together more and more often. These meetings can be the occasion for high-level discussions of corporate strategy; and they will be held not just in one and the same place but in various locations, again contributing to the strength of the group.

2

The Joint Boardroom

EXECUTIVES RUB SHOULDERS

The public bathhouse symbolised the communal nature of traditional Japanese society. There the local people would meet, not only to wash but also to talk or gossip. Today, with the rise of nuclear families and the preference for family privacy, the communal bath has fallen out of favour. In the corporate organisation, however, Japanese businessmen are used to working together in a large room filled with desks, rubbing shoulders with colleagues in different parts of the organisation. Almost every workplace consists of one large room where the office staff works. In contrast, in the United States and Europe, the offices not only of each department or section but often of each individual are usually separated. The Japanese office, though it may seem disorganised and clamorous, is open and flexible.

However, once Japanese executives are promoted to director-ships or above, they usually get separate rooms. The higher their position, the less often they come out of their rooms and the less contact they have with colleagues and subordinates. As they move up from director to executive director, to managing director, to vice-president, and finally to president, the bigger and more splendid are their rooms. As presidents or chairmen, in many cases they sit in an inner sanctum in the most secluded part of the head office building from which they control the company.

Some companies have realised that putting top management into separate rooms reduces the flow of 'bottom-up' information and dampens communication between executives at the same level. Few have gone much further in remedying the problem than simply to leave office doors open. Most presidents, chairmen of the board or other executives are too taken up by the mystique of their private offices to give them up. The result, inevitably, is less communication within the company, and the organisation becomes sluggish and bureaucratic.

The joint boardroom system at Honda is a rarity among Japanese companies. It means, as the name implies, that all the thirty or so executives of the company have their desks in one room. They meet regularly to discuss all kinds of matters. As they often go away on business trips, it is rare for all to be present at the same time. Ordinarily, most of them, including the president and vice-president, are on the move, on the lookout for fresh information that will help them in their work. Directors who are responsible for keeping the company abreast of the competition in the car or motorcycle markets are finding out about developments at Toyota, Nissan, Yamaha and Suzuki. An executive director may be making the rounds of domestic assembly plants to discuss and straighten out technical or personnel problems while a managing director may be calling on overseas plants to settle details of an investment plan for increased production. But should an emergency arise (such as the oil crisis in 1973) or should an important decision have to be made (such as on the plan in the mid-1970s to build a plant in the United States), they are all brought back to the one common office.

In response to top management questions such as What is the greatest problem Honda now faces? or What must we do in order to deal with changing conditions in the international, social or technological field? many projects are suggested, planned and carried out within each of the company's divisions following the 'bottom-up' pattern. Proposals are refined in the joint boardroom – some of them being what Honda people call 'big projects' – and executive or managing directors and other executives take the lead in putting them into effect as big project leaders (BPLs).

This method did not come about by chance; it was the result of a thorough and careful study of the role of an executive by Honda's top management who were freed from their responsibilities as divisional or regional chiefs. (Today, some directors are simultaneously divisional heads.) The executives work together not only on their own projects but to improve working conditions by paying regular visits to places of work, be they sales departments, factories or various departments within the head office.

Honda executives themselves say that the joint boardroom system is the best method for dealing with fundamental questions such as What should an executive do? or What is corporate management? and also for swift and decisive planning and decision-making by top management.

TOWARDS TEAM LEADERSHIP

The joint boardroom system was introduced in 1964 on the advice of Takeo Fujisawa. He believed that wide discussion of common problems would lead to sound decisions. Fujisawa and Sōichirō Honda seldom appeared in the boardroom but other executives later made improvements based on experience. The joint boardroom eventually became firmly established but only after a prolonged process during which different approaches were tried out, and as the result of which executives came to understand the proper role of management.

The oil crisis of 1973 coincided with a major change of leadership at Honda and this became the occasion for a bold experiment with the role of the joint boardroom and of the individual executives. That year, both Honda and Fujisawa retired. They had mapped out the way for the company, inspiring others to follow their example, and they could see that their task was completed. Once only a small workshop, the company had grown into a large concern with more than twenty thousand employees. Honda and Fujisawa realised that it could no longer continue to be managed in their way. What convinced them both to retire at the same time was that the younger men who had shared the hardships and challenges of the early days had now matured into fine businessmen. It was the joint boardroom which had been the training ground for these younger executives.

When Kiyoshi Kawashima (b.1928) succeeded to the presidency in October 1973, he recognised that the company had to move on from the leadership of individual genius to collective leadership. The time was ripe to make full use of the joint boardroom system.

TRIAL AND ERROR

In May 1973, a group of committees was set up, and through these committees, each executive was required to give serious thought to management, focusing on one of the three major managerial resources – manpower, materials and money. This was the beginning of a long period of experimentation and can be divided roughly into three phases as follows:

1. *May 1973–May 1979*
   Committees were set up to study matters relating to materials, money and manpower. In order to broaden their managerial perspective, each board member was assigned to one or other of the committees.
2. *June 1979–May 1981*
   In addition to the committees, four task forces were formed to improve executives' understanding of marketing matters.

Each force was headed by a managing director and dealt with one of four regions, namely Japan, North America, the European Common Market countries and Oceania, and the developing countries. The task force was a forum for wide-ranging and detailed discussions of market strategy.

3. *June 1981*

The committees and the four task forces were dissolved and replaced by six 'centres' with the job of formulating sales strategies for each segment of the world market – domestic two-wheeled vehicles, domestic cars, power products (domestic and overseas), North America, Europe and Oceania, and the developing countries. This reorganisation was aimed at making the best use of the executives at the front line of each market, applying what they had learnt about management and marketing in the committees and task forces.

These changes coincided with greater internationalisation of Japanese enterprises. A sense of urgency filled the joint boardroom. Honda had to move towards a more global system of management; it had to go beyond the 'localisation of production' (building plants in other countries and employing local workers), to the 'localisation of management'. Its efforts in this regard took the form of two major projects, the construction of a car plant in Ohio in the United States, and the tie-up with a major British motor-manufacturer, British Leyland.

In August 1979, Honda had opened a motorcycle plant in Ohio, and in December that year had signed an agreement with British Leyland for licensed production and technical collaboration. At the beginning of the 1980s, it was decided to construct a car plant adjacent to the motorcycle factor in Ohio (which began operations in November 1982). The tie-up with British Leyland bore fruit with the production and sale of the Honda-designed car, the Triumph Acclaim, in Britain (beginning in October 1981). The June 1981 reorganisation of the joint boardroom was carried out with the next two decades in mind, and marked the start of Honda's move towards global management. The company confirmed the following decisions:

1. In order to establish a strong foothold in the world market, the corporate drive will be made under the slogans, Concentrate on Sales and Make Honda Distinctive.
2. The president and vice-president will share responsibility for medium and long-term strategies while the rest of top management will attend to medium-term (three-year) plans.
3. The committees and task forces will be abolished and a system of six 'centres' established, each responsible for medium-term plans with regard to sales, profits, inventory, and investment in each market region.
4. Board members not serving as centre chiefs and vice-chiefs will assist each centre by taking charge of specific activities. Directors assigned as divisional heads will also participate in the decision-making of top management.

The new centres resemble company divisions, functioning virtually as separate enterprises; each has clear-cut roles and responsibilities to facilitate decision-making. However, the centres were prone to the sectionalism that stems from the vertical routes of communication in the divisional system. In order to counteract this and to promote horizontal communication and prevent 'tunnel vision', executives were put in charge of activities that cross divisional lines such as production technology and quality control.

Sectionalism is not a problem at Honda. In the joint boardroom, the president's leadership and the easy communication between the executives allow everyone to think and act freely: and this very freedom makes them aware of their responsibilities and authority as the company's top management.

CORPORATE GIVE-AND-TAKE

One may wonder why the early committees of the joint boardroom were focused on such broad categories as manpower, materials and money. Simplistic as they may seem, these categories represent the basic management resources, and it is a kind of management rule at Honda that executives, whether communicating with one another or with the company's employees, should always do so in ways that are as simple as possible. The broad reach of the committee's concern was important because it meant that the lines between the different categories of management would not be sharp and definitive. No matter what the task in hand, it had to be undertaken through the perspective of more than just one committee: the three would have to work together.

Any top-level problem in a corporation is bound to be complex. To build or remodel a factory, for example, decisions must be made about the size of the factory (material) and its location (material); what products (material) are to be manufactured there; how many workers (manpower) will be required; what will be the cost of the investment. All these matters must be looked at in terms of the interests of the company as a whole. What is even more important, however, is to have accurate information and understanding of world market trends (taking the competition with major rivals into account). Thus each of the three committees and the joint council of all three had to operate at a highly strategic level.

The joint boardroom makes it possible for the executives to exchange ideas and opinions freely, both on a formal or informal basis, regardless of their particular concerns. Only the chairman of the board, the president, vice-president and managing directors have desks and chairs of their own. The other executives take up positions at the table assigned to their committee for discussions with fellow members or sit at another committee table to discuss matters of mutual concern. There is also an unassigned table to promote free discussion among the executives.

All manner of ideas and problems are discussed in the joint boardroom. In its free atmosphere, which promotes in-depth exchange, some important decisions have been made. Examples are the cessation of light-weight car manufacture in October 1974 (production was resumed in September 1985 with the 645 cc. engine, Today), the construction of the Kumamoto factory for the production of motorcycles for export, the construction of the factory in Ohio, and the agreement with British Leyland.

In deciding to cease the manufacture of light-weight cars, for example, the survival of Honda as a fully-fledged car maker was at stake. The compact Honda Civic had been put on sale two years earlier, in July 1972, and in December of the following year (right after the first oil crisis) the company put on sale the Civic with the revolutionary CVCC engine which was designed to meet the Japanese anti-pollution laws. Doing away with light-weight car production, in which Honda was then a market leader, was a bold step aimed at allowing the company to concentrate on compact cars.

In dealing with this strategic issue, the committee on materials first discussed the future of light-weight cars and their sale potential on the world market. How did production of light-weight cars stand in Honda's business as a whole? Would continued manufacture jeopardize the all-out effort to expand the production of compact cars? One question led to another. The members of all the other committees were brought into the discussion.

The discussion was not confined to the executives in the joint boardroom. Employees working in the field on sales, in manufacturing and in research and development were called in for their ideas and opinions. The executives also went to listen to what ordinary workers had to say. The fact that light-weight car production was then a very profitable line of business for Honda made the decision all the more difficult. It was necessary to measure the capacity of sales, engineering and research and development and to judge how the cessation of light-weight car production would affect that capacity.

Honda analysed all its business divisions and product lines in terms of market maturity and product durability, and then considered the current state and potential of the light-weight car market. Its ultimate decision to suspend production was mainly based on the judgement that although in Japan light-weight cars were suitable in urban areas and might continue to enjoy a steady demand in some segments of the market, they would not have sufficient appeal overseas to become the company's main product. But above all else, Honda's executives realised that in order to remain a major car maker in the world market, the company had no option but to concentrate its energies on compact car production.

Withdrawing from a major line of production can lead to losses but stopping the production of light-weight cars turned out to be the right decision. Regulations concerning the maximum size of light-weight car engines were changed in August 1975 from 360 cc. to 550 cc., and with greater competition among car makers and traffic congestion in urban areas, the value of light-weight car production later increased considerably. But the profit Honda might have obtained by carrying on with it was far outweighed by its advance into the world compact car market.

In decision-making in the joint boardroom, Honda's executives attach great importance to the process of research and analysis, starting out with a free exchange of views from many different standpoints and sifting through ideas and arguments before arriving at a final decision. In other words, all the executives are encouraged and expected to speak freely. The relationships among the committees and their members are like those in a baseball team. During a game, it is sometimes necessary for the third baseman to catch a ball that is struck into the shortstop's defensive area. Likewise in the joint boardrom, lines of responsibility are not strictly marked out: each executive is directly concerned with an area defined by the committee or task force but no one needs to be afraid to enter other territories with their views and questions.

How do Honda's executives really feel about this way of doing things? Each is a strong, confident individualist and so one might expect them to feel offended should their area of jurisdiction be invaded and to be at one another's throats over conflicting interests. However, this is not the case. Honda executives know how important it is to be broad-minded enough to give a fair hearing to the views of others. The occasion calls for discipline and develops a kind of 'dynamic humanism' which means 'being sympathetic and considerate in dealing with others and at the same time acting with boldness and imagination'. This quality – unique not so much to Japanese tradition as to Honda's – was exemplified in the partnership of Honda and Fujisawa.

THE JOINT BOARDROOM AT WORK

What kind of discussions go on in the joint boardroom? Kiyoshi Kawashima, second president of Honda Motors, who took the lead in creating many of the company's original management systems described them as follows:

> We did not talk about serious things all the time. We might be chatting about the US presidential elections one moment and passing remarks about young people's fashions the next. Our conversation may wander considerably but it always comes back to topics close to and relevant to the management of Honda. Like college students, we often simply 'rap'. Some topics which other people might take for granted, we find ourselves arguing over for hours. And what is always uppermost in our minds are our responsibilities as executives and the proper course for company growth. Once we get on to one of these topics, we can go on for hours. No matter what we talk about, the subject always comes back to Honda and its future.

The joint boardroom is a forum where Honda executives pit their differences in a constructive way. It is not easy to recognize the good qualities of a person with a different speciality or style, but each executive knows that these contribute to the value of teamwork and leadership.

During this period, each subcommittee would organise its conclusions or findings into a plan that was presented to the board of managing directors before a final decision was made. Later, the task force system came into being, and from that time until the creation of the present system of six centres, the methods and process of decision-making by top management have remained basically the same. Rapid changes were taking place in the external conditions affecting the company's management and one of their difficult challenges was the friction between Japan and the United States and between Japan and European countries concerning Japanese car exports and the problems of local production. Other matters of concern were exchange rate fluctuations, sales and car fashion trends in each country, and, more recently, the application of electronics to cars.

The executives gather information on whatever the issue in hand happens to be (both in Japan and abroad) and invite specialists from inside and outside the company to furnish details. Armed with fresh information and expert advice, they return to the boardroom for a full discussion of each topic. As mentioned earlier, Honda-style discussions are frank and open; discussants talk until they are satisfied that they have a thorough understanding of the problem. They attend to what may seem to be trifling matters while being careful to see the whole picture. They do not hesitate to bring up any issue even though it may not be an urgent one – and especially if they think it may call for a prompt decision in the near future. Any topic, no matter how minor, is open for discussion at least once in the joint boardroom. The leadership of the joint boardroom is assumed by the president. The president is responsible for the final decisions on major issues but he has to be a good listener, adeptly drawing out the best in each of the executives and promoting understanding between them.

As was noted earlier on, not all the executives are always in the joint boardroom at any one time because they spend time on outside work. The directors and executive directors arrange their schedules to ensure that there are some executives on call at all times. Even if they are not all there, the room is usually alive with discussion. On some occasions the president may keep away knowing that his presence may inhibit frank discussion of some sensitive issues such as price competition in sales, troubles on the factory floor or transfer of personnel. He has to gauge the atmosphere of the boardroom and to judge when it is important to be present or not.

'Bold and careful' is the phrase used to describe the current president, Tadashi Kume, and his predecessor, Kiyoshi Kawashima. Both made it a rule in dealing with any problem to take a broad perspective without overlooking points of detail. They also take special care to try and draw out the individual talents of their subordinates. Having all the executives together in the same room is important but leadership is also vital to make the team run smoothly, and it is here that the managerial talents of the president are put to the test.

Kume says: 'If a free atmosphere is not maintained, fresh and novel ideas will not be forthcoming. The willingness to alter perspectives is important though it is not easy for company executives to break away from conventional modes of thinking. In Honda's joint boardroom it may seem at first glance as if everyone is jabbering away about this and that but it is precisely through this kind of free discussion that prompt decisions are reached. The kind of people at Honda do not have to be prodded by others in order to get things done. Since its founding, the company has got into the habit of moving into action quickly, no matter what the task. There are few cases in which they have to cope with factors they have never come across before. Most problems that arise are those they have already talked about at one time or another. Their most important decisions relate to the right timing for action.'

HORIZONTAL COMMUNICATION

In the typical corporate organisation it is rare for executives to meet all together for a frank discussion or exchange of views. Executives are usually attached to a particular division or branch of the organisation. Vertical communication is smooth but horizontal communication very difficult, and the problem is aggravated when divisions operate on an autonomous basis.

Corporations may try to promote horizontal communication but it is hard to ward off the drift towards bureaucratisation. The divisional system is an effective way to streamline management when the company is growing but the vitality of the organisation is difficult to maintain if the activities of the divisions are not co-ordinated. A key to successful management is to provide arrangements for horizontal links between divisions or departments.

Takeo Fujisawa was thinking along these lines when he proposed the joint boardroom idea in 1964. He realised that a corporation, as it grows, tends to become organisationally overstratified, and this leads to bureaucratism. He was determined to find a way to avoid this at Honda. Looking around, he saw that none of the younger managerial staff in the company seemed the least bit concerned with the workings of the company as a whole; as heads of company divisions or departments, they were absorbed by their own day-to-day affairs.

Fujisawa decided that the young lieutenants who were in a position to succeed to the company's leadership ought to be brought together and given the opportunity to discuss questions such as What is management? What should an executive do? What should our company do? and so on – not as heads of their divisions but as fellow members of the top management. That, he claimed, would not only stave off the bureaucratisation of the organisation but also contribute constructively to the future of the company. As long as everything was going well, no discussion among the executives seemed necessary, but after several management crises during the late 1940s and the 1960s, Fujisawa realised how important it was for executives to discuss basic issues that would emerge in times of adversity.

The joint boardroom came into existence, then, as a means of getting round the aversion most executives have to talking to one another and the bureaucratism that follows. Finding ways to reverse this tendency is a managerial challenge. Obviously, discussion among managers is necessary but even in private corporations there is insufficient dialogue among top executives. The tendency to withdraw into one's shell – and to keep ideas and opinions to oneself – is typical.

American methods of management have had a big influence on Japanese corporations since the end of World War II. Many books on management by American authors have been translated into Japanese and widely read in Japan. Many of the authors have visited Japan, making the influence all the stronger. Among them is Peter F. Drucker, management consultant and educator, and is probably one of the few who still enjoys a high reputation in Japanese business circles. In his book, *Management,* he states that managers must always be aware of the question What is my business? and they should examine it when the company is doing well. Too often, it is not until a company is in difficulties that management realises the importance of such basic questions.

According to Drucker, there are good reasons why management prefers not to discuss the question. One is that the question is likely to trigger off argument, counter-argument and discord. Posing the question brings out the differences within top management. It comes as a shock to these people, who believe they know each other well because they have been working together for many years, to find that they often do not agree even on basic issues.

Not only in the American corporations which Drucker describes but in most Japanese companies of large or medium size, executives rarely take the time to talk things through.

Perhaps they think the time has long passed when a discussion of fundamental questions can be meaningful or useful. But as Tadashi Kume has warned, honest and open debate among executives only begins by questioning everything that has been taken for granted in a company. The frank exchange of views that takes place in Honda's joint boardroom has broken down the inhibitions against better communication between executives.

UNIQUE VIEW OF PEOPLE

The success at Honda in removing the barriers that separate members of the top management stems from the way its executives see other people. In their approach to human relations they begin on the premise that each individual is unique and that there are bound to be differences between individuals. Recognising these differences, Honda executives seek to bring harmony out of conflict while respecting each other as human beings. It is on this account that they do not suffer the shock Drucker describes as common to most executives of suddenly realising that they and their colleagues do not share the same perspectives or outlook.

Seeing how Honda's joint boardroom encourages the free exchange of views, some companies have tried to imitate it, but most have not been successful. It is easy to copy something in form but not as easy to capture the spirit that makes it work. Any attempt to adopt the joint boardroom system is fruitless and pointless without an appreciation of this spirit.

The president plays a vital leadership role in the joint boardroom. It is he who speaks up when everyone else is silent. He is careful not to talk too much but helps to keep things going. It bodes ill if all is quiet.

Drucker states that while executives should speak up on the question What is our business? he admits that this can be hard for them to do since they like to keep to themselves.

Executives have their opinions, of course, but they are reluctant to air them and to hear the opinions of others.

Japanese executives generally think of themselves as 'men of action', and attach more importance to practice than to discussion. They are admirable for their ability to look ahead, move forward, and, when times are hard, even look backward – but they seldom look sideways. Men of action are capable of powerful leadership in a competitive world; they are assertive and ready to set an example. Without these qualities, the people under them might not follow them. Sectionalist organisations allow executives to reveal their talents as 'men of action'. The greater the sectionalism, the more effective they appear. But this is a vicious circle that must be broken. Honda's way is to have all the executives put aside from time to time the concerns of their own divisions in order to consider the management of the company as a whole. Each company, of course, must take its own history and style into account in the attempt but then commit itself fully to whatever method it adopts; half-heartedness will get it nowhere.

Almost all successful business leaders, in Japan and elsewhere, are people who are able to view and analyse themselves and their enterprises objectively; they are able to put themselves in the other person's shoes and to see things from other people's point of view. If executives are hesitant about listening to others and taking part in free discussion, it is usually caused by the bureaucratism that has taken hold of their organisations. As managers, they should always be aware of the interests of the company as a whole, and yet as heads of particular divisions they may be so preoccupied with their specialisms that they fail to see the overall picture.

For the Honda executives, their specific concerns are important but they also have the opportunity to be part of a total management structure. Their consideration of the 'general' is not constrained by their understanding of the 'particular'; the one complements the other. They visit sales outlets both at home and abroad and go to see for themselves how the relation of men and machines in the factory differs from country to country. With first-hand information, they return to the joint boardroom well equipped for vigorous and meaningful discussion. Information and ideas are pooled and experiences shared for the common benefit.

Honda's Joint Boardroom

The committee system was set up in May 1973 and the task forces added in June 1979 (see figs 1 and 2, pp 104-5). The committees and task forces were abolished in June 1981 and the six-centre system created.

In August 1985, the boardroom moved to Honda's new office headquarters in Tokyo. The six-centre system remained unchanged. The joint boardroom became square in shape and larger in size (see fig. 3, p. 106).

3

The Complementarity Principle

Armed with the three essentials of sound business strategy –
thorough preparation, meticulous planning and capacity for
bold action – a company takes on risks in the pursuit of profit.
Not all its projects go according to plan; some are successful
while others are abandoned on account of unforeseen events.
In some cases, success comes only after getting over one
difficulty after another. Business means taking risks and
success is hardly ever guaranteed. A company should therefore have some kind of safety net, and this should be seen as an
essential part of management strategy.

Honda's safety net is to have a complementarity policy in
product development, marketing and personnel management.
Risky ventures are balanced by less risky ones; executives who
are daring and sales-orientated work along with those who are
more cautious and technology-orientated; a bold innovation is
backed up by solid know-how. The complementarity principle
evolved out of many years of experience; to see how it evolved,
it is useful to look at some events in the history of the
company. From among the management crises, major and
minor, that Honda has faced over the years, let us look at two
examples.

One was the sharp drop in exports to the United States that
took place in 1966, presenting a grave crisis for both the
parent company and American Honda Motor, the subsidiary

set up in Ohio in 1959. Sales of almost all Honda's products, including the Super Cub which had been selling steadily for a long time, came to a virtual standstill in the second half of 1966. The other crisis was the controversy over Honda's mini-compact car, the N360, which came to a head in June 1969. This model had been selling well until complaints were made that the car was defective, and sales then plunged.

Honda learned a great deal from these set-backs and one important lesson was the need of a safety net for management. The new management strategy was created to deal with immediate problems and was then fleshed out over the years from practical experience.

THE AMERICAN CHALLENGE

Although Honda does not seem such an oddity as far as enterprises go today, this was not always the case. Its non-conformist tactics often got the company into unexpected difficulties, bringing it close to bankruptcy more than once. In each case, however, some opportune change came about in external circumstances that worked in Honda's favour, enabling the company to ride out the crisis. Such was its good fortune that people began to wonder if Honda was perhaps divinely protected!

The experience of selling motorcycles in the United States in the 1960s was one example. American Honda Motor had been set up in June 1959 to sell motorcycles in a country where the car was so dominant that there was practically no motorcycle market. The Japanese economy was just beginning to grow quite rapidly and some felt that Honda was risking a great deal in its American venture. Most companies would have started off by developing the South-east Asian market since it seemed easier to penetrate and was closer to home. But Takeo Fujisawa, Honda's chief of marketing, was no ordinary entrepreneur. If motorcycles were to capture a world market, he said, they had to be accepted first in the United States, the consumer economy par excellence. Any product that passed muster in America could be called the genuine article. Fujisawa had long dreamed of challenging the US market in this way, and the time had surely come.

Fujisawa's partner, Sōichirō Honda, had taken a 'global perspective' from the very beginning and had worked to make products that would be acceptable in any market in the world. He enthusiastically supported Fujisawa's proposal for taking on the US market for he, too, had been waiting for the day when he could put his motorcycles to the test of international competition.

The speed with which the two men took on this challenge provided the impetus for the growth of Honda into the world enterprise it is today. Never ones to take the easy way, they did not hesitate to accept the most difficult odds though that sometimes brought the company to the brink of a crisis.

Being reluctant to leave the job of breaking into the American market to a trading company, Honda formed the American Honda Motor Company so that it could do the selling in the United States. The market for motorcycles at the time was limited to sales of about 60,000 units a year. US motorcycle manufacturers, even Harley-Davidson, were relatively small enterprises. The main demand for motorcycles came from police forces, the only other customers being motorcycle gangs or clubs. Into this market, Honda brought the Super Cub C100, introduced in Japan in August 1958. It was a different sort of motorcycle from the heavy machines, being lightweight with a 50 cc. engine. Honda aimed at people travelling short distances, students on college campuses and housewives doing errands. Honda targeted the ordinary, mass consumer – not the bike freak – and sought to create a completely new market for the product which would overlap little if at all with the existing market. This approach was a resounding success.

In the space of five years, Honda succeeded in creating a

major new motorcycle market in the United States. The following figures give an idea of its phenomenal rate of growth: in 1960, about 6,400 units were sold; in 1961, 26,700; in 1962, 77,700; in 1963, 126,200; in 1964, 191,800; and in 1965, 444,700. In half a decade, the American market had grown seventy times and seemed set to keep on expanding.

The development of an American market also helped the company's growth in Japan. In 1965 Honda's main business was still motorcycles. Their sales then came to 93.4 billion yen, 75 per cent of Honda's total sales of 123.7 billion yen; the remaining 25 per cent was of four-wheeled vehicles, including light-weight trucks, the S500 and S600 sports cars (12%), cultivators (9%) and parts (4%).

Honda's earnings from exports to the United States grew along with Honda's success in the market there. In 1965, its total production of motorcycles stood at 1,465,700 units of which 688,800 were exported; of these, 444,700 went to the United States – 64 per cent of all Honda's motorcycle exports and 30 per cent of its total output.

Honda built its American market from scratch and exports to the United States rapidly became one of its mainstays. The dream, however, was not to last, and in 1966, sales to the United States dropped to 121,900, less than one-third of the number sold the previous year. By 1970, the American market had virtually dried up. This unexpected set-back presented Honda with a very serious problem since the company had thrown its full weight into this sector of the business. Stocks piled up at an alarming rate. Three hundred thousand motorcycles sat unsold, a number equal to almost three-quarters of Honda's sales the previous year! This was a measure of the crisis facing the company. Cash flow was tight and the possibility even of bankruptcy could not be ruled out.

All the signs had pointed to Honda's continuing success in the United States but suddenly the entire venture was on the verge of collapse. Takeo Fujisawa was in charge of sales and finance at the time and Kawashima had built up the American market. The situation called for cool but prompt analysis so that appropriate measures could be taken.

The Vietnam War had grown from a civil war in a small country in South-east Asia to a major conflict. The United States was committing itself more deeply to the war every day and this had repercussions not only on the US economy but on the world economy as well. Honda's motorcycle sales reached their peak in 1965 but this was also the year US President Johnson began to escalate the war and Fujisawa and Kawashima believed that this escalation brought about the start in the fall in the demand for Honda motorcycles. The US economy as a whole was healthy but many of the young men who had been Honda's main customers were being drafted into the armed services. These men were finding it more and more difficult to purchase consumer durables, including motorcycles, on credit, and, with the prospect of being sent to Vietnam, they were less interested in buying motorcycles, or even much of anything else.

The downturn in sales, however, could not be attributed entirely to these events. Fujisawa and Kawashima had to accept the possibility that Honda had misread the signs and had failed to keep up with changes in the market. At the time, Volkswagen was doing very well with its popular Beetle car precisely because it had not been changed. Honda had perhaps become complacent because the Super Cub was selling so well at home and abroad. Obviously, the ideal product for a company is one that does not need to be changed and continues to do well against the competition, but this cannot go on for ever. People eventually do want a change. In market economies, companies have to keep abreast of changes in consumer preferences and try even to anticipate them. On this reasoning, two things had to be done: one was to dispose of the excess stock and the other was to develop new products in response to market changes.

Model changes were made to the Super Cub and sales slowly began to pick up. The excess stock was reduced by slashing prices and throwing in accessories. The crisis at American Honda Motors had affected the parent company in Japan too and the company learnt some useful lessons from the experience.

Meanwhile, quite another factor was working in Honda's favour, namely, the growth of sales in South-east Asia. Ironically, motorcycle sales in war-torn Vietnam were rising rapidly. This turn of events will be discussed a little later on.

MANAGEMENT FOR GOOD FORTUNE

Developments in the mid-sixties helped Honda to get itself out of a difficult situation. But no company should rely on luck; it must try to protect itself against unforeseen adverse events. Honda's top management found out – though by chance – how indispensable a built-in safety net can be for the survival of a business.

In this instance, Honda's top management discovered the 'complementarity principle'. The drop in motorcycle demand in the United States was offset by expanding demand in South-east Asia, a fortunate complementarity between different markets. It is not surprising that top management began to think of applying the concept of complementarity to other aspects of the business.

No matter how bad business may become, it is hardly ever quite hopeless. There are always some positive signs; human beings have a way of finding a silver lining to every cloud. Corporate management that has the right spirit of entrepreneurship is always actively on the look-out for new markets and the heads of companies in a declining industry must be especially alert to promising new fields. Some products do not easily attract consumers while others sell so well that production cannot keep up with demand. It is management's job to distinguish between the easy and the difficult markets and treat them as mutually supporting for the benefit of the company.

THE MUTUAL SUPPORT SYSTEM

The situation in Honda's US and South-east Asian motorcycle markets in the mid sixties – in which losses suffered in one were balanced by gains in the other – became the prototype of Honda's pluralistic marketing strategy. Each country has its own unique cultural and historical heritage so that market conditions vary a great deal, and each market has to be judged differently. The more countries and markets a company works in, the more effective is the principle of mutual support or complementarity. Honda's top management believed that safety nets could be built by having complementary structures in various parts of its enterprise. The basic elements of complementarity which Honda later accepted through its experience and which the company used in its management strategy can be summed up as follows.

1. Motorcycles and Cars

The complementarity principle is well illustrated in the relationship between motorcycles and cars. Indeed, this point is not shared by other major car makers such as Toyota and Nissan or by motorcycle manufacturers such as Yamaha and Suzuki. Honda Motors began as a motorcycle manufacturer but Sōichirō Honda wanted the opportunity to challenge the small car market.

In the decade during which Honda took up that challenge – from 1963 to 1973, from the light-weight T360 truck and the S500 sports car to the popular Civic car – the company relied on its motorcycles for they had won a reputation by that time. The mainstays of the company's car production during the period were the mini-compact N360 and the light-weight Life car. Even then, there was a complementarity between the motorcycle and car divisions of the company. Top management noted the potential that this seemed to promise.

Motorcycles and cars are both vehicles with elaborate

engines but they are quite different machines. Cars with their increasingly complicated electronic devices and other highly advanced technology are becoming more and more remote to the ordinary user. On the other hand, motorcycles give their riders a feeling of greater control and more contact with the world around. But while the two are quite different kinds of products, they are closely related technologically and functionally, and so it is not at all strange that they should be seen as complementary products. Between them, the two-wheeled and four-wheeled vehicles can provide a strong 'safety net'.

As external economic conditions have become more complex, the complementarity of motorcycle and car production and sales has proved to be more and more valuable for Honda. For example, when the exports of motorcycles to the United States fell during the recession there in 1975, Honda was able to increase its exports of the Civic car which it had just introduced to markets both at home and abroad. Honda's total exports to the United States actually rose despite the recession. What turned out to be instrumental in securing the stability and growth of Honda's business, however, was setting up the Ohio plant in the United States.

At that time, building plants in the United States was an issue of interest to Japanese car and motorcycle manufacturers. They realised early on that there would be a ceiling to the exports of their finished products, and they could foresee it would be necessary to invest directly in the United States, build plants there and hire local workers. Indeed, the rise in the number of Japanese cars exported to the United States and the European Community had begun to offend these countries, and it became imperative to resolve this problem not only for individual companies but for Japan as a whole if further growth was to be achieved.

Honda became the first Japanese car manufacturer to build a plant in the United States because it had already built up the world's strongest motorcycle division. Its first step was to set up a motorcycle plant in Ohio and to gain the experience of production and management in that country. This minimised the risks for the company when it opened its adjacent car plant.

Honda's major rivals in motorcycle manufacturing, Yamaha and Suzuki, were not much interested in building plants in the United States: though Yamaha had localised motorcycle production in the United States, it did not make four-wheeled vehicles; and though Suzuki was producing cars domestically, it did not have the resources to risk an off-shore production venture. That Honda had both two-wheel and four-wheel vehicle divisions (strictly speaking, there is a third division of power products) stems from the entrepreneurial spirit of its founder. His successors, Kiyoshi Kawashima and Tadashi Kume, followed suit, grasping the special characteristics of the motorcycle and car markets and developing the complementary relationship between the two types of vehicle in the context of the corporation's total global management.

2. Domestic and Overseas Markets

Another illustration of Honda's complementarity policy is in the relationship between its domestic and overseas markets, between domestic sales and exports. Even during the period of Japan's rapid economic growth from the latter half of the 1950s to the early part of the 1970s, there were times when domestic markets were sluggish, and it was especially during these periods that management became more attracted to expansion overseas. Their efforts, however, began in earnest as the domestic market reached saturation point and Japan's economic growth slowed down.

The Japanese motorcycle market had reached a kind of maturity in the mid-1960s, and during the following decade there was intense competition for larger shares of the market. The growth of the motorcycle industry was largely dependent on overseas markets until the mid-1970s when Honda created a new domestic market aimed at making motorcycles a household item. The first model for this market was the Road Pal, put on sale in February 1976 and designed for women to use.

Meanwhile, Honda's motorcycle division has established three distinct types of supply: sales of finished products in the domestic market, exports of finished products and off-shore production (including kit production, that is to say, assembling parts supplied from Japan). Each of these three types came to roughly the same amount – about one-third of Honda's motorcycle production in 1980.

It was not easy for Japanese manufacturers to produce more finished products, to increase exports or launch off-shore production ventures exactly as planned, because of the complexities of local government policies. Be that as it may, the three types of supply show different characteristics and Honda took advantage of them thereby making the company less vulnerable to macro-economic trends and the ups and downs of local economies.

The oil crisis of 1973 provided the opportunity for new developments in the domestic market and in the global strategies of Honda's four-wheel vehicle division. Once again, the concept of mutual complementarity greatly helped Honda, though a late starter in the car-making business, to increase its share in the world market at a rapid pace and establish a place for itself there.

In October 1974 Honda announced its decision to suspend production of light-weight cars for by that time sales of its compact Civic had become firmly established. Overseas demand for light-weight cars at that time was negligible for there was then little concern about energy conservation and intra-city use. Honda had been Japan's largest maker of light-weight cars but it decided to abandon their production in order to concentrate all its management resources on making a success of the Civic. The decision stemmed from the fierceness of the competition in the four-wheel vehicle market and the difficulty of securing a place there. Honda sought to maintain relations with their customers of light-weight cars, offering the Civic as the next step up in a compact passenger car. Honda took advantage of its experience in light-weight car production in the shift to compact cars, and its success is proof of the shrewdness of Honda management.

3. Regional Markets

A third dimension of the complementarity principle is the relationship between the markets of the different countries to which Honda exports its products. The best example is the company's experience in the mid-sixties when (as already described) sales began to decrease in the United States and to increase in South-east Asia.

Honda is a global corporation exporting to 150 countries all told. It also engages in off-shore production in 39 countries by direct capital investment. On both counts, Honda is among the top Japanese manufacturers. Each market has its own historical and cultural features; they are not uniformly influenced by macro-economic trends nor do they respond to them in the same way. Within Europe and South-east Asia, there are countries with different political and economic systems as well as distinctive cultures. Countries also differ in terms of economic and social development. Studying the characteristics of each country and its market enables one to identify the significant differences between them as well as ways in which they might complement each other.

Take Europe for example. A comparison of European Community countries shows that each has a unique history of motor-cycle and car use and that the characteristics of each country's vehicles do differ: not only are they distinctive in design but in many standard features. The external economic policies of each country are often also different so that market accessibility is not the same. It would be unwise to regard the European Community as one market – each member country calls for close analysis and a marketing approach tailored with great care.

It is precisely the variety of countries that allows Honda to use the complementarity strategy to best advantage. Honda's exports to European markets in recent years have not fluctuated uniformly nor have fluctuations in one product coincided with fluctuations in another product. The company's export and marketing strategies must therefore be diverse.

COMPLEMENTARITY IN MANAGEMENT

It is a long-standing belief that an organisation – whatever its form or function, private or public – should have a single leader or head who is in ultimate command and takes all major final decisions. Two heads, it is said, cannot work together. Honda is unusual in that it was for many years a corporation with two heads. Sōichirō Honda and Takeo Fujisawa were equal partners in terms of roles and responsibilities but their personalities were quite different – the frank, outgoing and progressive Honda seeming to take the lead, the more reserved and shrewd Takeo Fujisawa playing the supporting role. In fact, however, their relationship was not at all one of boss and subordinate.

True, Honda was president and Fujisawa vice-president; the former was officially superior to the latter. But in actual work, they were equal partners; their relationship was essentially complementary and supportive. Intervention by the vice-president in the authority of the president was never a problem for each appreciated the strong points of the other. In this instance, two heads were better than one.

Honda was not all that familiar with finances or sales, but knew that Fujisawa was; Fujisawa, in turn, recognised his own limitations in the field of technology, leaving Honda to take charge of the development of new products. Both knew that together their respective talents could mean success. Their personal relationship was one of mutual respect though it was not always smooth and easy. A forceful personality can attract some people but repel others. Both Honda and Fujisawa had strong personalities but were aware of the need to tone down their more abrasive differences. This 'two-headed-eagle' leadership continued for twenty four years until Honda and Fujisawa retired from active management in October 1973.

Another example of 'two-headed' management was Sony in its early years. Sony became established during the rapid growth of the Japanese economy under the leadership of Masaru Ibuka and Akio Morita. Both were outstanding engineers but Ibuka took charge of research and development while Morita worked on the market front. Ibuka and Morita were inseparable partners but there was a 13-year age gap between them and (as symbolised by the later transfer of presidency from the elder Ibuka to the younger Morita) their relationship was a 'vertical' one between senior and junior. Honda and Fujisawa, on the other hand, had a 'horizontal' relationship working side by side as equal partners.

Another major Japanese corporation is Matsushita Electric (known abroad for its National and Panasonic brands), founded by Kōnosuke Matsushita. During the period when he was the president of the Matsushita group of companies (until 1961) and even after he stepped down to become chairman of the board (until 1973) and later executive adviser, he remained the group's owner. His relationships with his right-hand man Aratarō Takahashi, with Masaharu Matsushita (now chairman of Matsushita Electric) and with Toshihiko Yamashita (former president of the company) were all vertical or 'boss-subordinate'.

The way in which Honda and Fujisawa led Honda Motors, making decisions on an equal footing, is quite exceptional. Come to think of it, every rule has its exceptions. As long as organisations are run by human beings, there will be different types of leadership but the experience of Honda Motors shows that it is possible for a company to have two heads and be successful.

Complementarity of leadership led to the concept being applied to other aspects of management. This approach allowed the company to marshall the minds and experience of all its management. At first glance Honda's management may seem to move forward single-mindedly, its advance seemingly monolithic and unstoppable, but in practice, a sense of balance is always at work within the organisation. This management 'safety net' has its origins in the principle of mutual complementarity which the founders recognised and translated into a practical management strategy.

HARDWARE AND SOFTWARE

Creative entrepreneurship which makes for technological innovations often leads to social change. The benefits innovations bring to society are usually welcomed but they may be the source of controversy. Honda's pioneering spirit in technology and its success in opening up new markets brought it face-to-face with the full force of the consumer movement.

The N-360, a light-weight car introduced in 1967, had a dramatic story. It was a car that was blessed and cursed at the same time, and it sparked off a crisis for Honda on the same scale as the sharp drop in exports to the United States described earlier on.

The N-360 had an air-cooled, dual-cylinder engine and front-wheel drive, a standard feature on today's cars but uncommon then. Its small 360 cc. engine was nonetheless capable of generating 31 horsepower; the car could reach a maximum speed of 115 kph. and climb an incline of 20 degrees, a performance equivalent to a compact car. It was equipped with a padded shock-absorbing steering wheel and other safety features. It consumed fuel at 28 kilometres per litre and sold for what was then the very low price of ¥313,000. The car sold like the proverbial hot cakes – about

650,000 in the seven years the vehicle was on the market. It was truly a car for the masses.

The smooth sailing was short-lived. There were, as with any other car, accidents involving the N-360, and in June 1969, a suit was brought against Honda on the charge that the car was dangerous. Sales began to fall sharply. Honda reacted in a positive way since improvements had to be made so as to remove all doubt about the safety of its cars as quickly as possible.

Honda's corporate organisation or cluster of human resources can be compared to a clock's pendulum. Its entrepreneurial spirit made the pendulum swing wide as it tackled new ventures and faced the risks. Honda had run into trouble before and the experience had given it some know-how. The crux of this know-how is the principle of complementarity, the prototype of which was the relationship between its two founders and between their unusual personal qualities. In the case of the N-360 problem, complementarity again made it possible for the company to ride through the crisis. The company pendulum could be left to swing vigorously but not recklessly.

On this occasion Honda fell back onto its campaign to promote safe driving and its on-going research on car accidents. The company had been giving classes in safe driving since 1962 at the Suzuka Circuit, a Honda race track, and 60,000 persons had attended these classes. Prompted by the controversy involving car defects, Takeo Fujisawa set up the Honda Driving Safety Promotion Centre in October 1970. Its purpose was partly to demonstrate that a car maker should not simply make and sell cars (the hardware) but offer instruction on safe driving as well (the software). When the N-360 controversy broke out in June 1969, the company had already shown its commitment to safe driving and had considerable data at hand on the factors that led to accidents. Honda undertook several surveys on accidents involving the N-360: it found that in the majority of cases, the drivers were either inexperienced or using someone else's car, and that such accidents were not unique to the N-360. The Driving Safety Promotion Centre cost money, but for several years the company budgeted 600 million yen for its maintenance (additional to personnel expenses) treating it as part of the total or social cost of car production.

The N-360 controversy provided a severe test for Honda's second generation leadership. The man who dealt with the problem and who came up with the idea of a driving safety promotion programme was Michihiro Nishida, then a managing director (later vice-president and currently an adviser to Honda). Takeo Fujisawa recalled events at the time in his book *Taimatsu wa jibun no te de* (*The Torch Is in Our Own Hands*):

Honda Motors recognised the need for safe driving and was offering driver education at the Suzuka Circuit. We gave instruction, based on practical experience, to licensed drivers. After the Diet hearings on the problem of defects in Japanese cars, Nishida put his proposal to the board of directors: 'We should not be content with practical experience but should supply accident and other statistics to scholars, experienced drivers and experts so that they can come up with scientific explanations about safe driving. If ways can be found to reduce human casualties, it is the responsibility of everyone in the motor vehicle industry to see to it that the necessary steps are carried out. It is a mistake for car makers to try and escape responsibility for accidents simply because people are licensed to drive. Today, Honda is not making any profit but I am most anxious to give this idea a try'. A large proportion of funds was set aside and the safe driving centre set up, and Nishida himself became its director.

The N-360 controversy badly affected Honda's reputation and profits plunged. By setting up the Safe Driving Promotion

Centre, however, Honda managed to offset the negative turn of events with a positive step to create new, favourable conditions.

BOLD AND INCISIVE DECISION-MAKING

In September 1967, six months after the N-360 had made its debut, the Honda F-1 racing car won the Italian Grand Prix. Honda used these two events to full advantage – improving its image as a manufacturer on the frontiers of technology as well as popularising the car. Honda was an enthusiastic participant in international car racing but also a manufacturer of good-quality, low-priced, lightweight vehicles. Its sales campaign in advertisements in major newspapers throughout the country at the end of 1967 focused on these two sides of Honda to great effect. One half of the advertisement showed Honda's winning Grand Prix racer and the other half showed the N-360 moving smoothly through the snow. The advanced technology symbolised by the Honda racer endowed the small popular car with the qualities of a high-performance machine, an association of ideas which gave good results.

Honda engines had an outstanding performance – not only for its racing cars but in its lightweight vehicles. Despite the small cylinder capacity of the engines, they produced many horsepower – the result of the technical ingenuity, effort and determination of Sōichirō Honda.

There are three ways to raise the horsepower in car and motorcycle engines. The first is to increase the engine's exhaust capacity by making the cylinders larger. The second is to raise the compression ratio of the engine for greater fuel-burning efficiency. The third is by raising engine revolutions, and it is this that Sōichirō Honda worked to perfection. It is difficult to say which of the three is the best method as each has its limitations. Increasing the engine's exhaust capacity is limited by the size of the car itself. Raising the compression ratio is difficult because it is related to the octane content of the fuel. Raising engine revolutions was not the easiest in technical terms.

Sōichirō Honda was the first to use overhead camshafts (OHC) to raise the engine revolution rate (although today they are in common use). He also made modifications to reduce noise and vibration. These efforts paid off and he succeeded in developing an engine with twice the revolution rate so that an engine say, of 50 cc. had the horsepower equivalent of a 100 cc. engine. This was an outstanding technical achievement.

The instant success of the N-360, the controversy about car defects that affected all the leading Japanese car makers in 1969, and Honda's establishment of its Driving Safety Promotion Centre – these occurred during the company's research toward increasing the horsepower of its engines and the top speed of its cars. Though a lightweight car, the N-360 engine performed with the horsepower and speed of a larger car.

The pursuit of greater speed had been a byword at Honda for many years and had had great appeal in the early 1960s. However, other priorities were then to shape the car market with the rapid spread of motorisation in Japan. The Honda Driving Safety Promotion Centre was one response to changing needs. In the latter half of the sixties, car safety, anti-pollution measures and energy conservation were becoming important social issues. It was time for a drastic rethink of policy and objectives.

A chapter in Fujisawa's book has the title, Forget About Speed. It describes how Honda's leaders – Sōichirō Honda, Takeo Fujisawa and Kiyoshi Kawashima – noted the subtle changes in the times and what they did to transform the basic assumptions upon which their company was managed. The account describes events in the spring of 1971, just before the introduction of Honda's new lightweight car, the Honda *Life*. The consumer movement was getting stronger and people were pushing for safer cars.

One day I read in the newspaper that the US government was introducing speed limits for cars, and it made me feel that the world was becoming critical of high speed. We at Honda needed to be aware of this. If we were not careful, we could easily become the scapegoat. The *Life*, with a new water-cooled engine and a top speed of 120 kph., was already on the production line. That very night, I talked over the matter with Kawashima, then managing director, by telephone. I told him I thought it would be more in keeping with the times to cut the *Life*'s top speed to about 100 kph. I realised that at a time when car makers were competing feverishly in the top speed of their cars, it would seem strange for Honda to come out with a car with a reduced speed. The popularity of our cars might suffer even more if people thought that we had cut down on speed because the N-360 was faulty.

Our selling points so far had been speed and design. What would happen if we threw away one of our trump cards? Would people still buy our cars? Facing this crossroads, it was even harder to decide on the right course to take. As I told Kawashima, I felt stymied; I did not know what to say. We could not wait for the return of Mr Honda from a business trip in the United States because documents had to be submitted to the Ministry of Transport and the deadline was upon us. Then Kawashima said, 'Let's go ahead and cut down the speed. The car will be easier to drive. It's better that way. I will tell the board of directors myself.' I was immensely relieved to hear those words and more convinced than ever that Kawashima was an astute decision-maker.

Speed had been a feature of Honda cars; reducing it might have worked to the company's disadvantage but continuing to make increased speed a selling point in defiance of the trend of the times would have been an even greater risk. That is how Fujisawa and Kawashima read the signs and their judgement (even though Sōichirō Honda was away at the time) led them to decide to reduce the speed of the *Life* in order 'to give the public what it wants'.

It is hard to imagine the difficulty of this problem for men like this, and their decision was all the more difficult because they knew it might hurt Sōichirō Honda's pride: it was he, after all, who had worked for a better, faster machine. What made it possible for them to go ahead with the decision was the principle of complementarity. The reduction in the top speed of the *Life* became for the two men a major experience in total management strategy. The next generation of Honda's top management, Kiyoshi Kawashima and Tadashi Kume, were likewise careful both to be optimistic about developments external to the company and to be sensitive to what was going on inside the company. They made it a practice to arrive at decisions only after taking account of the diverging views presented to them and looking at problems from every possible angle.

WARP AND WEFT

Takeo Fujisawa describes how he arrived at his basic management philosophy in the following way in his book:

A scholar of classical Chinese literature, Kojiro Yoshikawa, once wrote that the first character in the word *kei-ei* (management) means *tate ito* (warp thread), and I think this provides a very useful insight. In weaving cloth, the warp remains stationary, running the full length of the piece of cloth. The second character, *ei*, then corresponds to the weft. Only if the warp is kept straight can the weft thread pass smoothly from side to side in creating the fabric. The warp is strong and continuous but flexible enough to incorporate whatever kind of weft comes along, depending on the circumstances. That, I believe, is the true meaning of management. In the first two years after founding Honda Motor Company, Sōichirō Honda and I used to talk by the hour. More than once we talked until three or four in the morning. The result of our long talks was the warp of Honda Motor, and I suppose that what gave it character was Honda's humanism and my romanticism.

The warp that runs through Honda is represented by the company's motto: 'From a global perspective, Honda undertakes to respond to customer needs by producing low-priced products of superior performance'. It is also the atmosphere within the Honda organisation that generates the vitality of its people who make a reality of ideas and ideals. With this solid, continuous warp thread in place, it is possible for the weft – its day-to-day activities – to move freely and flexibly. The relationship of warp and weft in the Honda management philosophy is conducive to imaginative and innovative ideas. It is the prototype of the complementarity that forms the basis of Honda's total management strategy. The implications of this approach are that:

1. Things are looked at from both the vertical (warp) and horizontal (weft) perspectives.
2. A multi-dimensional grasp of the existing situation underpins planning for the future.
3. Horizontal decision-making mechanisms are an important aspect of the company's management.
4. The organisation is designed and operated in a flexible fashion so that project teams and task forces can be put to tackle specific needs.
5. Both individual freedom and organisational cohesion are necessary, and are given equal priority in the corporate structure.

The division of responsibility of Honda's top executives forms a matrix, making the best of complementary relationships and promoting individual initiative and team strategy.

As the joint boardroom management style became established, it greatly contributed to the company's growth and stability. The company's entrepreneurial spirit might lead to taking risks designed to make the company grow, but management crises could also be kept to a minimum.

RISK MANAGEMENT AND COMPLEMENTARITY

For many years after the company was founded, Honda and Fujisawa led the business by instinct and feel; their extra-ordinary leadership kept it running smoothly and vigorously. The time came, however, when they realised that a formal organisational framework was needed, and that they should retire from active management. They recognised that the younger men who had helped them build the company were now ready to take over and put their own ideas into practice. The organisation, moreover, had grown complex, and lines of communication, chains of command and the functions and responsibilities of the various sections within it had to be made clear.

By the end of 1973 when Honda and Fujisawa retired, the company had become a large-scale organisation. While sales had been ¥124 billion in 1965, they had grown three-fold to ¥367 billion by 1973. From 1975 on, Honda grew more rapidly than most other car manufacturers. After 1985, its sales had reached ¥2 trillion, and today it is on the way to ¥3 trillion.

The retirement of the founders coincided roughly with the difficult times of the first oil crisis. The entire Japanese economy was shaken by the crisis, and enterprises without sound strategies for survival soon fell by the wayside. Honda's new generation of management had been trained to manage 'with a global perspective'; now they had to learn to read the changes that were taking place and make decisions to ensure that the company could survive the crisis. The younger generation of Honda's executives understood the management rule that 'the larger the company, the stronger it is to withstand external adversity'. They applied the paradoxical principle that taking risks could actually help to ensure the company's stability.

Comparing Honda in the mid-sixties, when it faced the crisis of the drop in exports to the US, with what it is today (as sales near ¥3 trillion), it is clear that the company is now much more stable. The growth rate of the company is slower and the advantages of scale are offset to some extent by the bureaucratisation that accompanies the increasing size of an organisation. These are disadvantages that must be accepted, but in terms of stability the company is far better off today. The basis for this stability is the total management strategy based on the principle of complementarity.

Taking risks is part and parcel of business. The biggest task facing management today is how to predict changes in internal and external factors and to minimise the risks of taking risks. But even the best management system fails occasionally. In the long run, it is better not to be afraid of risk-taking but to build up an organisation that can withstand the shock if something goes wrong. This is what risk management is all about.

With subsidiaries all over the world, risk management is common practice at Honda. Locational risk stems from many different factors – political, social, and so on. Dealing properly with each is no easy task. Unexpected developments arise from time to time and factors that seem at first to have no bearing on a situation may turn out to be closely connected with it. Forecasts may turn out to be wrong and this can be the source of mistaken decisions. As we have seen, here is where Honda's complementarity principle proves its worth. Complementarity allows the company to ride small failures and cope with large ones, and hence maximise net gains and successes.

One example of the difficulty of forecasting locational risk is the story of Honda's sales in Nigeria. Africa had been unexplored territory for motorcycle sales, but following the first oil crisis, demand for motorcycles grew steadily in many parts of the continent. Honda exported 84,900 motorcycles to Africa in 1975 and 98,300 in 1976; in 1977 the figure leapt to 163,000. The prosperity that made this possible was partly the result of rising Nigerian exports of oil to the European Community and in particular to the UK. Honda had begun to study the African market and to work out new strategies for its development. In 1978, however, sales collapsed to 15,500 units, one-tenth of the amount in the previous year.

The direct cause was the sharp drop in demand in Nigeria. Sales there came almost to a full stop as a result of the crisis brought on by a sharp drop in sales of crude oil to the UK. Developments in the North Sea oil fields had started to affect Nigeria's economy adversely and the effects were felt, in turn, by Honda in Japan. Who could have thought of this at the time?

Every global enterprise should recognise the importance of prudent and far-sighted management strategies that will enable unforeseen risks to be minimised. For Honda, the answer is its proven philosophy of complementarity. During Kiyoshi Kawashima's term as president, between 1973 and 1983, Honda stood ahead of Japan's car industry in its global strategy. The company's direct investment in the United States was its response to a new dimension of risk management, and (as explained earlier on) it was its total management strategy that provided for stability and growth.

Tadashi Kume, third and current president of Honda, also relied on the complementarity 'safety net' in expanding production facilities for motorcycles, cars and engines in the United States and in building the car plant in Canada. The 'safety net' is now strong and reliable, allowing the company to take risks fearlessly and to move confidently on to new ventures.

4

Individual Play and Team Strategy

The Honda Research and Development Company was led personally by Sōichirō Honda for years while the management of Honda Motors was left largely to his partner, Takeo Fujisawa, and his staff. Devoting himself full-time to R & D, he worked closely with the staff at the two centres in Wakō and Asaka in Saitama prefecture from the time of the company's founding in July 1960. This personal leadership enabled him to pass on his ideas and experience and to lay the foundation of Honda R & D as the 'brain' of the Honda Motors group.

By April 1971, when Kiyoshi Kawashima took over the presidency of Honda R & D, its role as part of the Honda group (as well as its philosophy) had been well established. The company was ready to move on from Sōichirō's personal vision and grow into a mature organisation. Kawashima had played a leading role in setting up the joint boardroom management system, and he was well placed to create an organisation and work out strategies and principles to guide the research staff.

All the parent company's research and development have been done at Honda R & D. At the end of 1985, the R & D affiliate had about 5,500 employees, working at three centres in four locations. Its job was to supply Honda Motors with blueprints for new product designs in their final form. The capital resources for this work has been supplied by the parent company and now amount to 5 per cent of HMC annual proceeds. As company earnings increase year by year, so the percentage allocated to research is increased, a policy that reflects the company's emphasis on investment in R & D. In 1980 Honda Motors' sales were ¥1,345 billion and 3.2 per cent (¥43 billion) was allocated to research. Eight years later, in 1988, Honda's annual proceeds stood at ¥26,367 billion and 6.6 per cent (¥1740 billion) went into research and development. In terms of the actual amount spent on research and development, Honda is still behind General Motors, Ford, Toyota and Nissan, but a 250 per cent increase in R & D expenditures over the eight-year period is an exceptionally high rate of growth.

Honda's aggressive efforts to develop new products for a wide variety of car, motorcycle and power machine markets (both at home and abroad) have also made the company unique among its rivals. The atmosphere at Honda R & D, as at other company affiliates, makes for the full use of each worker's talents. How is this atmosphere created? The answer is found in the policies that feature respect for individuality, encouragement of self-training and competition among employees, carefully co-ordinated teamwork, readiness to take on big projects, and quick responses to urgent problems. It is these policies, together with the company's unique research and development system, that have helped Honda Motors to take and hold the lead in the world market.

Taking over the leadership of Honda R & D from Sōichirō was an exciting challenge and a heavy responsibility for Kiyoshi Kawashima. The company's style of management up until then had given the staff a great deal of freedom without much in the way of organisation. The management had made 'zero controls' their goal but now that the company had grown so large in terms of work force and sales, rules had to be made and a formal organisation set up. How to continue with the atmosphere of freedom and keep the crippling effects of bureaucracy at bay were problems the new management had to tackle.

Each of Sōichirō's successors as president of Honda R & D – Kawashima (April 1971–June 1977), Tadashi Kume (June 1977–June 1981), Hideo Sugiura (June 1981–December 1984), and Kazuo Nakagawa (December 1984 onwards) – shared the belief, passed on from one to the other, that at Honda R & D, 'human psychology is crucial'. Anyone who is head of a group of forceful personalities must have regard for psychological factors in order to build an effective team and ensure that individuals give of their best. Honda R & D's organisational chart is not pyramidal but horizontal, the overall scheme being designed to encourage individuality. This means that the president and other executives must keep in touch with the feelings, opinions and needs of each member of the organisation.

The leaders must also keep the organisation flexible and adaptable to changes in external circumstances. They have to keep abreast of market demand, current and projected, and this relates to consumer markets of many different kinds. Another task is to maintain constant contact with HMC sales staff in Japan and abroad and to know about the requests and advice of dealers. Management, executive and research staff make it a rule to get out on the sales front line where they can get the feel of events firsthand. They have to be able to tell when the old should give way to the new; when one technological generation must give way to the next. They sow the seeds of new products and nurture them until the time is ripe to put them on the market. The most important aspect of the entire process, however, is the leader's ability to understand the thinking of the researchers and bring out their talents.

KEYS TO HONDA LEADERSHIP

Both Kawashima and Kume served in the top position at Honda R & D before assuming the presidency of Honda

Motors. Their succession was approved by one and all for several reasons. First, to keep the spirit of innovation alive within the whole Honda group, HRD's head must be familiar with technology and open-minded as a businessman. Second, Honda's research and development are based on market-orientated pragmatism. Third, the presidency of Honda R & D is itself a kind of trial by fire; any executive tough enough to handle its challenges must surely be able to take on the management of Honda Motors. Fourth, although we cannot say that only an engineer is qualified to head Honda Motors, the job of president would be too much for someone familiar only with sales or finance. For some time yet, the presidency of Honda Motors will continue to be filled by successful past managers of Honda R & D.

Honda R & D presidents each developed their own approach while in office. Tadashi Kume was known while he was president (1977–81) for his cryptic expressions. He used to say that the keys to Honda R & D success were 'madness', 'an old fox', 'moon rockets' and 'the gods'. The research personnel at Honda R & D must have an irrepressible pioneering and innovative spirit. People who are wholly determined to reach some goal are bound to appear a little crazy to others.

To lead a group of 'mad' engineers, a supervisor must be as shrewd as 'an old fox'. He has to be quick to understand the moods and attitudes of the researchers, pampering them when they face disappointment, restraining them when they become impetuous, supporting them when they have personal problems. In other words, he stands ready to offer timely assistance to the individuals as and when it is needed.

When Kume was HRD president, the greatest achievement in advanced technology was landing the first man on the moon in 1969, through the teamwork of the NASA staff. Kume talked about 'moon rockets' to illustrate the kind of teamwork researchers have to learn. They had to have individual initiative (where real technological advances begin) but also to be able to work in a team so as to bring projects to fruition.

When Kume talked about 'the gods', he was referring to the sense of justice and impartiality that are required of the researcher as well as of the manager and the executive. A project may not be profitable but if the idea is one that responds to people's needs, researchers should pursue it to its conclusion. Environmental pollution, toxic exhaust fumes, energy conservation – at first, problems such as these may seem insurmountable but no problem should be seen, in principle, as impossible to solve. How close researchers come to solutions depends on their organisation's commitment to doing what is right – perhaps transcending short-term profits – and on their individual conviction that problems can be solved. Knowing that what they are doing contributes to a better world – that they are not just working in a vacuum lifts the morale of researchers and gives point to their work. Research and development carry a moral content.

Puzzling as Kume's symbols may be, they make good sense, and this shows how thoughtful the president of Honda R & D must be, sensitive to the psychology of the engineers and staff. He must respect individuals and their creative endeavour, and at the same time mould them into a successful team.

Another of Kume's ideas was that as a leader, a company president does not always have to be in the vanguard or take the initiative. In the light of business realities today, it is often more appropriate for a president to be a co-ordinator who is alert to the interests of the staff. Kume once said that a president needs the many talents of a professional geisha. Geisha are alive to the individual traits and preferences of their clients, and while a geisha may now and then display her own talents, she spends time building up a warm and pleasant atmosphere for her guests.

Kiyoshi Kawashima, Kume's predecessor, also saw his role as president in the spirit of a host or hostess entertaining guests. He aimed for an organisation where the engineers could freely express their feelings and be themselves. He believed that outstanding achievement would blossom naturally in such an organisation. Kawashima's successors have treated management on the view that an engineer is a human being first and a technician second.

Honda researchers try and keep their thinking young and fresh and in tune with the ideas and ideals that first stirred their imaginations. Kume elaborated on this as follows:

> The driving force in the growth of an enterprise is ideas. At the R & D centres, priority should be given to ideas over technology since technology is the crystallisation of ideas. Sōichirō Honda's 'global perspective' is my guide, and we must respect the demands of theory and ideas in creating products that will be welcomed by people all over the world. This is the true mission of Honda R & D.

In any big organisation the individual can easily be submerged by the whole. At Honda R & D, management strives to uphold respect for the individual and individual values.

THE SED SYSTEM

The organisation and functions of Honda R & D are shown on page 107 (fig. 4) and a picture of the development system given on page 108 (fig. 5). The first headquarters of Honda R & D were built in Wakō, just north of Tokyo, in December 1961. This is the 'mecca' of Honda research and development. In October 1973, another centre was built in the nearby city of Asaka. This coincided with the retirement of the founders as well as the first oil crisis. Motorcycle research and development moved to the new centre. In May 1979, the Asaka East R & D Centre was set up to take charge of research and development for Honda's power equipment products. Though this division carries less weight in the overall Honda scheme, Honda's engine technology is used to the full in the production of agricultural machinery, and these have often become pioneers in the discovery of new markets. Thus, the R & D system is responsible for the three products – cars, motorcycles and power equipment – and this upholds the system of mutual complementarity at Honda Motors.

The transfer of the car R & D centre to Tochigi began in April 1979 when Honda opened a proving centre with a test course in Tochigi. In April 1982, under the supervision of the Wakō Centre, the new-product development division was moved to the Tochigi Proving Centre, leaving the Wakō centre to concentrate on basic research. The Honda R & D system was now more or less completed. How did these centres go about their work?

Among the ideas Kawashima used while he was Honda R & D president was 'simultaneous competition among different approaches'. This remains the essence of the Honda R & D method today. The central questions for Kawashima were: What is the best way to bring out the talents of each researcher? Is there a way of getting optimum teamwork so as to beat the competition within a limited period of time? How can we make it possible for employees to enjoy their work and get a sense of fulfilment from it? Kawashima developed the idea of 'simultaneous competition among different approaches' to suit the character and spirit of the company, making it the guiding principle of research and development as well as a practical tool for getting things done.

THE CHALLENGE OF THE CLEAN AIR ACT

The way the principle of 'simultaneous competition among different approaches' works is well illustrated by the development of the CVCC engine in the early 1970s. It was a time when the damaging effects of industrialisation were beginning to be felt in countries such as the United States where air pollution had become a big issue. In December 1970, the Clean Air Act (popularly known as the Muskie Act) came into effect, most attention being paid to eliminating car exhaust fumes. As with many trends that originate in the United States, the air pollution problem soon became a major issue in Japan. Here, there is far less space than in the United States and factories are heavily concentrated in certain areas and as the number of cars was growing rapidly, the need to do something about toxic emissions and wastes was urgent. In October 1972, Japan's Environmental Agency (acting on a report from the Central Environmental Pollution Counter-measures Council) published a Japanese version of the Muskie Act. In December 1974, the Council submitted another report, Regulations on Car Exhausts, which stated that air pollution could be eliminated only through the initiatives of car makers. The report stated that the amounts of carbon monoxide, hydrocarbon and nitrogen oxide in car emissions would have to be cut by 90 per cent.

The new laws came as no surprise to Japanese car makers, but Honda was the first to get on with research that had actually begun before the Muskie Act was passed. In the end, Japanese car makers achieved more impressive results in elim-inating toxic exhaust than their counterparts in the United States. Their success, in fact, greatly enhanced the com-petitiveness of Japanese cars in the international market.

Honda's top management began seriously to tackle the pollution problem in early 1969. They knew the company would have to develop a 'clean' engine. In the joint board room (which was by then fully operational), it was unanimously agreed to make anti-pollution/clean-engine research a top priority. While other car makers were still discussing the problem, Honda got on with concrete research.

In its approach to this work, as with any other, Honda R & D followed its practice of putting a number of individual researchers to work on the problem and letting them compete to come up with ideas for its solution. The first stage was to field all kinds of proposals from among the research staff. Then a series of projects were begun on the various proposals to test their feasibility. In the area of fuel supply, for instance, it was suggested that catalysis and reactor systems might lead to a cleaner engine. Exhaust-gas recycling was another possibility. All of these would require changes to the existing engine. At this stage, attention was concentrated on a basic study of combustion as well as on research on gas turbine motors.

A cleaner engine was the first major theme adopted in the 1970s by Honda R & D's Research Evaluation Committee, a small member group made up of the president, other top executives and supervisors representing both the engineering and non-engineering staffs. The committee gave the go-ahead to all research projects that promised progress towards the clean engine. The entire organisation went into action, the researchers excited by the opportunity of showing what they could do. Research on ways of devising a clean engine was sanctioned for both individual staff and project teams. Many different approaches were followed at the same time, thus ensuring maximum diversity.

Here we may note another of Honda R & D's watchwords, namely, 'one theme per person or group'. This means that a theme of one researcher (or group), once approved by the Research Evaluation Committee, cannot be taken up by anyone else. This leaves the field open for many different tracks towards the same goal. With rare exception, most proposals are accepted in order to encourage freedom in research. Themes are taken up on the understanding that they may have to be abandoned at any time at the discretion of the Evaluation Committee. Nevertheless, the system is different from assigning a number of researchers to a single theme.

To illustrate the difference, suppose that one engineer starts research on a catalysis method for a clean engine. Another engineer, who has been engaged in a basic study of combustion, examines his colleague's work and may conclude that it will not come to anything. Rather than criticise, he leaves the problem of deciding whether the study is sound or not to the

Research Evaluation Committee. He is free to submit to the committee his own idea using a different catalysis method, a thermal reactor method, or whatever else he thinks will work. If his theme is accepted, he can start working on it even though the other engineer may still be engaged on the previous theme. The one-theme-per-person (group) approach is part of the 'simultaneous competition among different approaches' principle – giving a lot of freedom to all of Honda R & D's engineers and providing an effective tool for encouraging creativity and originality. The personalities of the engineers differ a great deal: some are 'seed-sowers' – having rich imaginations and coming up with a succession of ideas; others are 'ploughers' – they painstakingly select a single theme and concentrate all their efforts on it alone.

Each of the four Honda R & D centres has a Research Evaluation Committee which includes not only engineers but persons familiar with sales, personnel management and international affairs. The composition of the committees shows the care that is taken to ensure that every aspect is taken into account. To offset the tendency of technicians to confine their studies to limited aspects of the problem, there are laymen who keep an eye on their work, but these must be people who believe in the project as much as the technician, have a critical insight and a broad vision.

The role of the evaluation committee is mainly to sift out the unfeasible projects so that only the most promising ones are taken up, bearing in mind the constraints of time and checking on the projects through successive evaluations. This process is illustrated on page 108 (fig. 5). It should be noted that a clear-cut distinction is made between research and development at Honda R & D. At the research stage, the committees decide on the themes to be given the go-ahead. If research is started on ten themes aimed at the same goal, the committee weeds out the less feasible ones, paring the number down one by one to the final theme.

Since the policy is to allow researchers to pursue any theme they want, the evaluation committee is not put off even if most of the themes it approves at the R stage do not come to anything and are not taken on to the D stage.

At the D stage, Honda R & D has the co-operation of the sales division of Honda Motors (S) and the engineering staffs of Honda Motors and Honda Engineering (E). Here is where sales, engineering and development converge, giving the SED system its name, and thereby merging experience with know-how to create some of Honda's most successful products – the Civic and Accord cars and the Road Pal and Tact scooters.

In sifting through research themes at the R stage, committee members have three crucial tasks: to determine how a theme fits in with the needs of society as a whole, contributes to the interests of the company, responds to the demands of consumers and helps advance technology; to help clarify the goals of the research themes; and to provide advice on how research should be carried out. Clearly, committee members have to be well informed about market conditions, both in Japan and abroad; they have to be creative and positive in their thinking in order to stimulate the researchers' imagination and keep their morale high.

CLEAN, NOT CLEANED UP

In developing a clean engine, Honda followed its traditional policy of seeking a solution by pioneering its own technology. In 1970, when Honda R & D began to look for ways to meet the anti-pollution challenge, Sōichirō set the direction of research in down-to-earth language. He said, literally, 'don't be nightsoil men!', that is to say, collecting waste and dumping it elsewhere. What Sōichirō was getting at was that a way should be found to avoid having to dump anything – to devise an engine that would not create any contaminating wastes in the first place. The crux of the emission problem is that the nitrogen oxide content of exhaust increases in direct proportion to the quantity by which carbon monoxide and hydrocarbon content are reduced, and vice versa. It seemed impossible to find a solution to this problem within the time available. Honda chose to restructure the engine itself (see fig. 6, p. 109).

In the catalysis system, toxic gas is treated only after it has already been discharged from the engine, and this involves the possibility that secondary pollutants may be formed. Sōichirō warned the HRD staff of the perils of such a solution. It was typical of his leadership style to set a goal, formulate a programme of action and carry it through to completion. Adopting a catalysis system would have meant acquiring new expertise in metal and chemical technology as well as introducing electronics technology for system control. The message Sōichirō was trying to convey was his conviction that the emission problem could only be solved by a mechanical restructuring of the engine to make it self-cleaning.

The result was the Civic engine. In this engine, the cylinder head contains two combustion chambers instead of one. A thin gasoline and air mixture is injected into the main chamber and a slightly denser mixed gas into the secondary chamber. The denser mixed gas in the secondary chamber is ignited first by the spark and the combustion spreads to the thinner gas in the main combustion chamber. The CVCC engine has three valves, two aspiration ports and one exhaust port. The temperature within the engine rises more slowly than that of older engines. The slower burning process results in the lower emission of toxic gases such as carbon monoxide, hydrocarbons and nitrogen oxides (see fig. 7, p. 110).

Almost all Japanese car manufacturers, including Toyota and Nissan, opted for a catalysis system, but Honda came up with a self-cleaning engine by altering the engine mechanism.

After the oil crisis in 1973, the Japanese economy lapsed into a period of slow growth and corporations started to dispose of their excess capacity and stocks, cut back on personnel and curtail borrowing. In subsequent years, the economy moved out of slow growth on to a growth rate that was higher than in other advanced countries. In this phase, the Japanese car industry was subjected to three major problems. One was the restrictions on car emission, a problem the industry had faced since before the oil crisis. Another was a new problem, the need to conserve energy, which stemmed from the third and final problem, zero growth.

Ultimately, the car industry triumphed over these problems. Japanese car manufacturers – shamed perhaps by the country's reputation as a haven for polluters – vied for new technology in the international arena. Though the anti-pollution laws seemed formidable at first, the solutions proved relatively easy in the end. The next hurdle – the need to conserve energy – was cleared by reducing the size and weight of both engines and chassis. The car industry resumed its remarkable growth within two years, and the techniques of quality control which were developed in the process of meeting the emission and energy conservation challenges gave them a distinct advantage in terms of international competitiveness. Now a symbol of Japanese-style management, QC (quality control) became a new dynamic force in the growth of the Japanese car industry and especially in the American market.

THE LABORATORY ON WHEELS

When Honda founded the company in 1948 there were more than ten other manufacturers in the motorcycle industry, most of them quite large concerns compared with Honda. In the latter half of the 1950s, the motorcycle market grew markedly as demand rose for a handy and cheap means of transportation: cars were still luxury products at the time. The number of motorcycle makers rose to about 100 but many of them were not much more than makers of bicycles. In the mid-1960s the number shrank to seven, and ten years later, to four – Honda, Yamaha, Suzuki, and Kawasaki. These four now hold an overwhelming share of the world motorcycle market.

Of the four, Honda was always the maverick – the least predictable and the most unconventional – and this image did not change even after it rose to the top of the industry. The person responsible for that image was Sōichirō himself who used to take part in races despite the physical dangers. He was also known for his passionate commitment to making motorcycles that people would enjoy riding. In the effort to satisfy the consumer and to cultivate new markets, he would take considerable risks and adamantly refused simply to imitate others. It was this spirit of entrepreneurship that enabled Honda Motors to overtake its rivals and gain a firm foothold in the world car market. The pivot of the challenge for Sōichirō was innovation and improved engine performance based on original technology. His ideals still form the basis for Honda Motors' philosophy of technology and underlie the company's approach to car, motorcycle and power equipment technology.

To Sōichirō, the symbol of high performance in an engine was high horsepower. There are basically three ways of increasing car or motorcycle power and speed. One is to increase displacement, and this requires a larger engine cylinder. Another is to obtain a higher combustion efficiency by raising the engine's compression ratio. The third approach is greater engine rotation speed, and this was Sōichirō's choice. Picking the simple orthodox solution was typical of Honda's approach towards advanced technology and, indeed, was considered so primitive that engineers had never thought of taking it up. Sōichirō began studying this method (which everyone knew about but no one had tried) as the natural thing to do. He soon acquired the necessary know-how and began to manufacture the engine on a commercial basis. After all, he was not just an engineer and inventor but an entrepreneur par excellence. The result was the N-360 lightweight car with the 360 cc engine that came on the market in 1967 (see p. 48).

When the N-360 was put on the market, Honda was still

more of a motorcycle maker than a car maker. The N-360 gave Honda confidence in its car technology and offered great promise in the lightweight car market. Like subsequent Honda cars, it incorporated the best of the company's R & D work. In the on-going search for better technology, Honda used the F-1 cars as a kind of 'laboratory on wheels' to test the limits of engine performance, chassis durability and strength, and many other functions. One of the greatest benefits of taking part in races was the boost it gave to engineer morale which helped to vitalise the entire Honda 'family'.

In 1985 Honda's racers won four Formula-1 car races out of sixteen races in the year – this was in Detroit, Europe, South Africa and Australia – a remarkable achievement considering that Honda had returned to full Formula-1 racing only the previous year.

Honda Motors took part in F-1 racing for the first time in January 1964. Its aim was to obtain data on durability, speed, safety and other factors under the severe conditions of F-1 racing. Honda was then planning to begin the mass production of cars and the data proved to be invaluable in developing the technology that was required. Honda's F-1 racer won its first Grand Prix race, despite great odds, in Mexico in October 1965. From then on, Honda racers won many races for both F-1s and F-2s. The know-how that was acquired from its 'laboratory on wheels' helped Honda to realise one of its important goals: to put advanced technology to use for the mass-consumer market. The N-360 was the fruit of that effort.

An F-1 racing car was something of a monster. It had an engine of only 1,500 cc that was nevertheless capable of 600 or 700 horsepower and even exceeding 1,000 horsepower. Such a vehicle not only tested the skills of its driver but the quality of every part of the car from the basic materials to the smallest component. For the engineers, the 'laboratory on wheels' put their technology to a merciless test.

Honda's F-1s were still on a winning streak when the

company abruptly stopped taking part in races in 1969, the main reason being that sufficient data had been obtained on increased horsepower through faster engine rotation. Another reason was the concern for safety. As the performance of racers improved and the horsepower of the vehicles grew larger, so the number of accidents increased. Honda management realised that continued involvement in F-1 racing would mean placing a higher priority on engineering than on safety, and this was a path it was not prepared to take.

The late sixties was the time when 'consumerism' was gaining strength in the United States, and concern for the safety of car users became a major issue in Japan as well. The anti-pollution laws of the seventies were their next challenge. Honda distinguished itself, as described earlier on, in the development of the CVCC engine.

The first oil crisis of 1973, however, presented the car industry with perhaps its greatest shock. Petroleum prices rose four or five times in a matter of months and this forced car makers all over the world to start thinking about economising on fuel. They had to find ways of making cars that would satisfy consumers who were conscious of the cost of fuel and the need to conserve energy. The countries without their own petroleum resources were hardest hit; Japan, then one of the largest oil-consuming countries, went through an especially severe crisis. Looking back, we now see that this experience became a springboard for the Japanese economy's subsequent leap forward. Every crisis in the post-war Japanese economy, in fact, forced businesses to seek new and better technology. As it turned out, the consumer movement, the anti-pollution laws and the oil crisis were all 'blessings in disguise' that forcibly pushed Japanese car manufacturers into a new era.

Japanese car makers in the 1980s have been so competitive as to create serious frictions between Japan and the United States and Europe. Honda Motors has resumed F-1 racing and one may ask, what does it have in mind? The twenty-first century is not far away; political, economic and social conditions are in a state of flux, and the driving force behind these changes is technological innovation. New, highly advanced technology is being developed all over the world and private enterprise will not survive if it does not keep up with events. Honda's F-1 racers, equipped with the newest materials and incorporating the latest electronic technology, are now playing a pioneering role in the development and application of highly advanced technology. The 'laboratory on wheels' is speeding towards the very different world of the near future.

5

Human Dignity and Efficiency

TOWARDS NEW MANAGEMENT NORMS

When Honda built its Kumamoto factory in June 1974, the company adopted a set of basic guidelines for the post-oil crisis era. As the results began to show in the company's performance, other corporations realised that Honda management had shown singular foresight. Honda's five guidelines were as follows:

Keep costs at a fixed level for a period of five years and develop a production system that would be profitable even if operations were cut back by 50 per cent.

Balance production efficiency with humane working conditions.

Save energy and conserve resources.

Seek integration with the local community.

Make preservation of the environment a major concern.

Consumers, individual as well as corporate, were shaken by the leap in energy costs, and industry in particular had to find ways to cope with very much higher petroleum prices. Absorbed by the immediate task of cutting costs and avoiding losses, many businesses simply put the future out of their minds. It was not surprising that Honda's guidelines, which were intended to cope with the difficult circumstances of the present as well as to keep an eye on the future, attracted attention.

The Kumamoto plant was the pilot project in the company's move to bring about a new thrust in its management. The guidelines spelled out the basic priorities in building plants through direct investment (domestic or overseas) with the aim of putting down permanent roots in local areas. These guidelines provided the overall framework for the globalisation of the Honda management system.

It is now established practice at Honda to provide what are called A00 (A-Double Zero) guidelines for each major project. These are the culmination of thorough discussions in the joint boardroom regarding the tasks the company must undertake. They are based on a critical appraisal of past management experience and an objective analysis of the current situation. In the early years, under the personal leadership of the founders, there was never the need for such broad discussion or explicit guidelines for management planning or decision making. Honda and Fujisawa had worked well together and they had been able to co-ordinate the activities of the company without hard and fast rules.

After Honda and Fujisawa retired in October 1973, the A00 guideline system was adopted to co-ordinate decision making and planning for major projects. In making decisions for action, the president and other members of the joint boardroom take into account what changes they think will occur in society and the economy, how internationalisation will affect the market as well as trends in world politics and economy over the next three to five years. Plans, for example, to design a new car or build a plant are made only after thorough study and discussion of these broader questions.

The next step is to make the plans more specific by drawing up what are called A0 (A-Zero) guidelines. These include the problem of market segmentation – the specific market to be targeted, the type and capacity of vehicle to be designed, the number to be manufactured, and so on. They provide details from the conceptual stage – the kind of vehicle Honda ought to market – through to manufacturing and to methods of sale.

We have already noted Honda's regard for theory, ideas and time. Founder Sōichirō believed the value of time had to be recognised and tried to instill in his employees a proper attitude in using it. When working out the nitty-gritty details of a project, Sōichirō emphasised the need to set the time required for an action programme. Projects should be such as to allow differences of approach or opinion but always within the given lead time. This was not an easy task, but it is made easier with sets of guidelines which help top management to work within a time scale.

There are also the guidelines which are detailed product development requirement lists. If, for example, a research team has decided to produce a 100-horsepower car, the list would include the specific technology required for an engine output of that size. The use of these A lists has now become an established practice at Honda.

THE WHOLE AND THE PARTS

The history of Honda's corporate development is marked with epoch-making new products and new plants. A company that can put on the market new products in response to immediate demand or such as to anticipate demand will capture the best opportunities for growth. It is no mean feat to time the development and manufacture of a product so that it comes on to the market when it has the greatest appeal. In chapter 4, we described Honda's SED system for the regular and successful development of new products. Of equal importance is the timing of new plants to fit into the process of product development.

The Suzuka factory (opened in Mie prefecture in April 1960) was built to manufacture the revolutionary Super Cub motorcycle and thereby making motorcycles accessible to the mass market. The Sayama factory in Saitama prefecture, completed in May 1964, signalled Honda's entry into the four-wheeled vehicle market and continued to be a major production base of its car divison. The Kumamoto factory (mentioned earlier on) was the first step to Honda's expansion into offshore production. It was also important in that it moved away from the 'quantity function' that had dominated industry in the period before the oil crisis. Everything had been keyed to quantity, production and consumption alike, and resources had been thought of as unlimited. The crisis brought industry down to earth and the ensuing slow growth forced it to reappraise its profligate ways and look for alternatives.

The Japanese economy had enjoyed rapid growth for so long that it was almost taken for granted when the first oil crisis struck in 1973. No one ever dreamed of zero let alone negative growth. Rapid growth, nevertheless, did end abruptly, to the surprise of government, business and consumers. Corporations began to respond by switching from the 'quantity' to the 'quality' function: streamlining their operations, curtailing the hiring of new workers, cutting down on excess capacity, and finding ways to use resources and time more efficiently.

Because Honda got the head start in this matter, it drew a lot of attention. Its basic approach was to find a way to maintain international competitiveness despite the fall in demand. Honda saw that international politics and the world economy were such as to make it difficult to keep on exporting cars or motorcycles as finished products. At that time Honda had already shifted its exports from finished motorcycles to knock-down parts in the South-east Asian markets and was in the process of launching local production ventures there. This readiness to adapt to a changing economic condition is indispensable to the continued growth of an enterprise.

Conditions are bound to keep on changing. This was only a few years before Japanese car makers had begun to respond to political and economic pressures by investing directly in the

United States, building plants there and hiring American employees. Honda became the first Japanese car maker to undertake offshore production, first the motorcycle plant and then the car plant in Ohio, and production facilities in Canada. The Kumamoto factory represented a new dimension in plant construction at Honda, designed as it was with the global market in mind. Even though it was located in Japan, it was conceived and built in such a way that it could be replicated in any part of the world and run efficiently. The fundamental guidelines for the Kumamoto factory – as stated earlier on – reshaped the company as an international enterprise.

TOTAL OPTIMUM

One feature of Honda's approach with new plants and other big projects is that the leadership is in the hands of executives of managing-director rank. For the Kumamoto factory, it was Shigeru Shinomiya (then managing director, and later pro-moted to vice-president) and he aimed for the best – in total terms, and no less for the future as for the present: his slogans were 'total optimum' and 'future optimum'.

As Shinomiya explained at the time the factory was being built, the plant might provisionally set its capacity at 50 per cent and hold costs constant for a period of five years in order to break even. This, however, could only be part of a wider target. Keeping down the cost of 'visible' operations in a factory may fail to take into account the 'invisible' aspects of management.

Transportation costs, for example, have to be considered in broader terms than simply the circulation of materials and goods within the factory. They must include the delivery of parts from suppliers and the movement of products from the plant to the ports at Hakata or Moji. For knock-down parts, costs would also include transport to factories in other countries, unpacking, assembly into finished vehicles, delivery to dealers and finally to the customer. Only by knowing about all these transportation costs would one have a proper statement from which to examine costs. Honda had found that the specifications for motorcycles were linked to the specific conditions of each export market, and this was relevant to finding ways to reduce distribution costs.

Shinomiya had useful ideas about 'the whole' and 'the parts'. The whole and its parts are relative; depending on the point of reference, the nature of the parts changes. For instance, if the market for a motorcycle is limited to the country of manufacture, the image of the whole is by and large defined by the various 'parts' of the domestic market. If we broaden the target market to include other markets, the 'parts' of the whole will change. Among the writings of West German physicist Werner Heisenberg (1901–76), the father of quantum mechanics, was the book, *The Parts and the Whole*. Heisenberg describes how scientists who work on the small units of matter will tend to overlook the order that governs the universe, the existence of God, the philosophy behind the material world and the spiritual world of man. They are so bound up with the parts that they fail to see the image of the whole; they do not see the wood for the trees.

Shinomiya's ideas about management are in step with Heisenberg's views. He repeated the warning that while it is important to attend to the bits and pieces of a business, it is even more important to have a grand design in the first place. This was in line with the beliefs of Sōichirō Honda and Takeo Fujisawa. Shinomiya explained that the construction of the Kumamoto factory began with 'the whole' and 'the parts' were then determined in terms of the whole. Finding the parts prior to the whole and forming the whole by simply piecing together the parts – this was not Shinomiya's way of doing things.

FUTURE OPTIMUM

According to Shinomiya, there has to be a 'future optimum' as well as a 'total optimum'. What does this mean? Take weaving, for example. 'Total optimum' corresponds to the woof, the threads upon which a fabric is made: it is the 'future optimum' – the time factor – that provides the warp. With both, a fabric will be strong and durable. Shinomiya's account of his experience at the Kumamoto factory echoes the experience of Honda from its earliest days.

The Kumamoto factory was planned and built chiefly by staff in their mid-thirties – those who would rise to executive posts in the next ten years or so. If we had given the project to the highly experienced staff in their forties, the factory would have been properly designed and completed swiftly, thus achieving a 'current optimum'. Getting the younger staff to build the plant meant that they would have to judge whether or not their work would stand the test of time. There was the possibility that their factory would be somewhat unrefined but it was likely to be filled with innovations assuring a 'future optimum'. In time, the factory would acquire one new look after another by virtue of its built-in capacity for adaptation.

This was the way Honda itself had evolved. Shinomiya joined Honda in 1951 (only a few years after its founding) and had been trained, especially in production, under the tutelage of Sōichirō himself. Teachers of traditional martial arts are known for the heavy demands they make of their protégés while giving little explicit guidance: it was up to individuals to find their own success. In the early days at Honda, the younger engineers had to tackle the assignments given to them by Sōichirō Honda by seeking the advice of their seniors, reading books, building things and taking them apart if they did not work, and otherwise coping as best they could.

Sōichirō's successors, Kawashima and Kume, followed the same technique.

Sōichirō had a way of dreaming big and throwing his ideas to younger employees who had the imagination and the know-how to turn them into reality. He gave his protégés a great deal of scope to 'do their own thing' even though this was a gamble on his part. The senior members of the company aimed to create an environment that would inspire younger people, nurturing ideas that would translate into practical technology.

The principles in Honda plant construction apply to all situations; they are no different for a factory built in Ohio or Kumamoto. One of the most important of these principles is the need to attend to those aspects of management that may be ignored but are essential for 'total optimum'. For example, in order to cut down on the transportation costs of the Kumamoto factory, it was necessary to look for advantages that would offset the disadvantages of its remote location on the southernmost island (Kyushu) of the country. Thus, the managers tracked the path taken by each part from materials to installation, gathered together all the shipping slips that changed hands in the process, and so located a number of 'control points' for each component. If, for instance, the materials for making a part were received and processed at the same place from which the part was shipped out, two slips would be needed to record the receipt and dispatch: the process involves two control points. It took a year or so to weed out the superfluous control points, but the result of these efforts was close to what the preparatory study had predicted.

Shinomiya also warned that those responsible for factory construction projects are concerned mainly with how to build a facility of a certain size by a certain date along with the machines and equipment. Being preoccupied with the hardware, it is unlikely that they will design a plant that makes adequate provision for human needs. Their building will provide for the smooth operation of machines but hardly for the proper use of human beings.

Problems like this have to be considered carefully at the planning stage, but preconceived ideas and traditional practices of management have led companies to ignore them. Some things, like control points, can be clearly and numerically expressed, but the operations of a factory depend not only on the movement of goods and the output of machines but on human relations, attitudes and behaviour.

The same principle can be applied to energy and resource conservation. Say, for example, that one per cent of the oil used on the machinery in a factory is spilled. This might be collected and burnt, be converted to carbon and cause no damage to the environment. For a one per cent loss, this solution seems good enough but what really calls for attention is the one per cent loss. Instead of seeing one per cent as very small compared to 99 per cent, we should think of it as large compared to zero; and we should try to find a way to reduce the waste to zero.

This example is one Shinomiya himself used to explain his approach and technique. He believed that, just as in a game of chess, business had to be conducted with the same regard for overall strategy and detailed tactics. Shinomiya played a leading role in planning the Kumamoto factory but his basic principles were shared by all the Honda managers carrying out specific projects.

The Kumamoto factory was up front in the drive to vitalise the company by expanding internationally (prompted by the first oil crisis). The factory became a landmark in Honda's expansion as the guidelines in its construction and operation became the principles of general company activities.

THE FREE-FLOW LINE

The head of the Kumamoto factory in its early phase was Takao Harada (now managing director). In terms of the overall company organisation, he was what Honda called a

Project Leader working under Shigeru Shinomiya, the Large Project Leader responsible for seeing to plants for the years to come. Shinomiya fed his ideas and schemes to Harada who then had to apply them in the management of the plant. It was Harada's job, moreover, to note the ideas and proposals of the young leaders in the new plant, and to co-ordinate their work. Last but not least, he had ideas of his own that he wanted to try out.

The guidelines required the plant to 'seek integration with the local community' and 'make preservation of the environment a central concern'. Dialogue between the factory management and local residents was therefore essential. In these matters it was the Honda way to work patiently and conscientiously, and this tradition was carried on by both Shinomiya and Harada.

Harada's concern was also to create the best possible atmosphere within the company. As the guidelines stated, the plant was to 'keep costs at a fixed level for a period of five years and run a production system that will remain profitable even if operations were cut back by 50 per cent', but this would not be possible without the second guideline – 'balance production efficiency with humane working conditions'. A major responsibility of the project leaders – then, now and in the future – is to provide a workplace where individual employees are motivated to work and acquire a sense of achievement.

An interesting feature of the Kumamoto factory is the 'free-flow line'. This is a production line designed so that the speed of production can be changed at will by the workers themselves. Honda was the first to adopt this system in the Japanese car industry.

At the time the mass-production assembly-line invented by Henry Ford was still the system of manufacture throughout the world. As comically portrayed in Charlie Chaplin's film, *Modern Times*, the speed of the conveyor belt is set by the management at what they judge to be the proper pace. The people working on this assembly line are at the mercy of machines. In the 'free-flow line', the workers can control its operation. On completing their task, they push a pedal that starts up the conveyor belt and moves the unit to the next place. The speed of the production line is determined by the workers themselves.

If the speed of a conveyor belt set by management is too great, the workers on the line grow edgy and psychological stress builds up. Numbed by the monotony of their jobs and alienated by the impersonality of the process, they lose all sense of fulfilment and motivation: far from achieving greater efficiency, the result is often an increase in the percentage of defective products.

This is typical of Honda's many attempts to make the production process more humane. The speed of the conveyor is set at a slower pace; coffee breaks relieve job monotony; teamwork and group tasks reduce the sense of impersonality and isolation of workers. Original ideas and inventiveness were also fostered through quality control group activities. Workers were encouraged to adopt a co-operative attitude towards others, each doing their work as carefully as if the product went directly into the hands of the customer.

Takao Harada (who supervised the birth of the free-flow line system at the Kumamoto factory) says that in remedying the faults of the traditional assembly line system, the main concern is how to give workers a greater sense of the intrinsic worth of their efforts. First, find out what makes a job worth doing and then figure out what makes workers dissatisfied. Harada and his staff considered many ideas which could give a sense of fulfilment to the worker whose job is confined to a limited part of the production process. They concluded that the best solution was to put the workers in control of the machines and let them determine the speed of the work. They could thereby work to the best of their ability at the tempo that suited them best.

The free-flow line had some initial drawbacks: it was longer than the conventional conveyor belt and more costly to install.

But it was held that the costs would be repaid if the system humanised the production process without even impairing efficiency.

PUTTING THE WORKER IN CHARGE

It was courageous of the Volvo Car Corporation to abolish the conventional assembly line as it did in 1974 and adopt the system in which each car is assembled from start to finish by a small group of workers. The decision to adopt the free-flow line at Honda, likewise, required flexible thinking and determination on the part of management. The usual approach would have been in terms of hardware, for example, increasing production by using robots. The 'soft' approach – putting the workers in control of the machines – would never have been proposed; and even if it had, the management would have vetoed it as being too costly. The way Honda adopted the system was typical of its brand of management where executives dare to try out fresh and original ideas.

Unlike the old conveyor belt system, the free-flow line provides three or four so-called idle stations between assemblers. When workers finish their particular job, they move the product on to the next idle station. In this type of system, an assembler can work very quickly and then take a break until the pile of units that has been passed on is cleared. In this way, the progress of the line is not disturbed as long as each worker keeps the next person on the line supplied with units.

In the conventional assembly line, conveyors move at a fixed speed, forcing workers to keep pace and denying them any leeway or freedom of activity. The new system gives workers some freedom. Using the button to stop or move a conveyor may seem to mean very little but it has a great psychological effect upon the worker. Under the old system, it was hard for people with different ways of doing things – right- and left-handers, for example – to work together. The strict procedures always put some workers under a handicap. With the free-flow line, workers can use procedures most suited to them. This gives variety to what is otherwise monotonous work; worker initiative is encouraged.

A conveyor belt set at a fixed speed gives rise to all kinds of stresses, not the least of which is poor relations with other workers. The speed of the line is usually set in accordance with the performance of the least efficient worker on the line, and this can only make the worker in question feel inferior and unhappy. More efficient workers may be frustrated because their efficiency is restricted by the less deft. These ill effects may be dealt with to some extent through quality control activities but these are more of a palliative than a cure.

Under the free-flow system, individual differences in performance among workers become even clearer, and how to keep the system running smoothly therefore remains a vital issue. Indeed, the role and responsibilities of the manager and supervisor are now all the more crucial. Identifying the particular strengths and talents of each individual and finding ways to put each to its best use takes on increased importance. Stresses and conflicts of a whole new sort may arise among workers but the merits of the free-flow line still outweigh the drawbacks. More humane and genuine relations among workers are achieved and this has given the work place vitality.

The adoption of the free-flow line at the Kumamoto factory was just one of the challenges taken up by the second-generation leadership of the company. It marked an important new phase in the growth of the company which was concerned with reducing the conflicts between human beings and machines.

At first the Kumamoto factory was engaged entirely in manufacturing motorcycles for export but later it moved into other lines of production which meant that the content of jobs was changed. Instead of turning out completed vehicles, it began to export partially assembled motorcycle units to assembly factories overseas. In turn, the growth in the exports of knock-down parts slowed down as full-scale production at overseas factories went up.

Under the new overall production plan of the Honda group, one third of production at the Kumamoto factory is now made up of motorcycle parts for export. Another third consists of motorcycles for the domestic market and the remaining third of agricultural machinery. Production and assembly line operations have been rationalised through the use of robots and other automatic equipment but regard for the worker-machine situation and working conditions remain fundamental priorities. The problems are as tricky and delicate as ever. The more automation is installed, the harder it is for the workers to feel satisfaction or fulfilment in their tasks. The old spectre of alienation has not been completely banished. The information society is already upon us and human beings are becoming immersed in communications equipment and high-technology. The challenge of preserving the authority of people over machines is one that industry must continue to recognise.

DIVISION OF LABOUR

The free-flow system was adopted at the Kumamoto factory as part of the overall effort to improve the quality of the working process and humanize production. The basic idea is that human beings should have some control over what the machines do and not the other way around. In other words, machines ought to make work fulfilling and satisfying, and the worker ought to do the jobs best left to human beings. By the same token, of course, those tasks best done by a machine should be left to the machine, thereby conserving human resources and utilising them to best advantage. When workers are made to do jobs that can be performed just as well by machines, the result is worker alienation, stress on the job and other problems. Tightening screws or crouching in awkward positions to install parts on a production line, for example, are not the best kind of jobs for human beings.

In building the Kumamoto factory, a survey of about 2,000 workers was conducted at Honda factories and this came up with some interesting results. Respondents were asked to identify the kinds of work they thought were 'demeaning'. The worst four were: carrying heavy loads, dirty work, detailed work causing eye-strain, moving or carrying things. The Kumamoto factory was then designed to free workers from these unpleasant tasks. Remote-controlled carts were used to carry loads from one place to another. To save the workers from lifting heavy loads, an automatically controlled warehouse system was designed to bring parts from the warehouses to the production line as needed by the assemblers in accordance with the 'just-in-time' procedure.

The free-flow system is not the be-all and end-all in humanising the assembly line. There are still ways the production line can be made more humane, and they must be sought out. Among the tasks for industry today is to study the nature of work, the man-machine relationship, human co-operation, and to think up better systems of management. Good management is an on-going process.

The ultimate aim of the free-flow system was to achieve the complete automation of assembly-line operations. One of the most pressing tasks in the car industry is to institute improvements and innovations that will revolutionise the assembly line, ultimately freeing human labour from all assembly work. What are the kinds of work that can only be done by human beings? The answer may be found through a careful examination of the jobs machines should take over. As the automation of the assembly line progresses, the human role has been changed to that of the monitor – watching to see that nothing goes wrong. Different as it may be from the drudgery of the old assembly line, even this is monotonous work and its negative implications cannot be ignored. The strains that pit human beings against machines have entered a more delicate phase presenting industry, management and worker with a new challenge to keep the production process within human control.

6

Hondaism Updated

OPPORTUNITY DEVELOPMENT

Top management should be constantly aware how their company stands in the industry and be fully informed about what is happening not only inside but outside the organisation. Indeed, a very important management job is responding and adjusting to changing circumstances and conditions.

It may happen, however, that while it is preoccupied with this or that development, management fails to give proper consideration to the interests of the people on the 'shop floor' and the fabric of human relations in the company. Caught up in the drive of quantitative expansion – whether it be to boost sales and profits by stimulating domestic demand or to maintain a given level of exports – management may overlook what the workers themselves think and want.

When a corporation is doing well and sales are increasing, its management may think it can just keep on as it is. Wages are rising and so it is thought that workers are happy. But this naive outlook is likely to lead to trouble. What needs to be done is to encourage workers' initiative and give them a greater sense of participation. Opportunities should be created to increase workers' motivation and draw out their talents.

At Honda, opportunities for its workers are developed in a variety of ways, notably through NH circle activities, the

Honda counterpart of the QC circles of many Japanese companies. The NH circle system now operates in the entire Honda group, and even in the companies and workshops associated with each local factory. In the mid-eighties, NH circles were set up in Honda companies overseas where they have produced remarkable results. The Honda group holds an NH circle convention each autumn to give selected circles a chance to report on their activities. In 1985, 84 circles presented reports to the annual convention, with 24 representing companies in twelve foreign countries.

Honda rejected the QC circle because it dealt only with cost reduction and quality control. Honda chose its own term, NH circle – N stands for now, new or next, and H for Honda – with a view to taking a broader approach. NH circles allow members to bring up any problem and provide a venue for discussing a wide range of subjects.

Emphasis on cost reduction leads to excessive concern with worker–machine or machine–machine matters. Often, it is the relationships between people that are crucial. Leaving room for matters not directly related to work brings about more lively and useful dialogue. The system allows workers to improve their interpersonal relationships and promotes closer teamwork, and this encourages them to raise questions of their own and to work together to find the answers.

NH circle activities are voluntary and worker-initiated; they help workers to 'get out of the rut' in their work procedures and to generate real interest in what they do. Not that the activities were aimed solely at promoting 'bottom-up' movement in the corporate organisation since they also improved 'top-down' communication and understanding. In any sound organisation there should be both bottom-up and top-down communication.

Honda's NH circles have more freedom than QC groups in other Japanese companies, and include the element of play in their activities. Honda is known for its 'Idea Contest' which is open to all its employees.

The NH circle and the Idea Contest along with the expert system, on-the-job and other training programs, the overseas trainee system, and the round-table meetings for top management and other executives – these are all ways of ensuring lively two-way communication at Honda. There is a 'virtuous cycle' in which information from the bottom flows to the top, and then passes back down in the form of proposals, recommendations and policies. In the absence of this 'feedback', data flowing from the bottom up could prove pointless.

THE NH CIRCLE

Leading corporations in other countries were quick to adopt Japanese-style QC circle activities and to study Japan's TQC management. With the internationalisation of both the Japanese economy and corporate management, Japanese businesses are obliged to put their TQC management and QC circle activities to the test in other countries. This is a great challenge.

Honda is already meeting this challenge in many parts of the world. The philosophy behind the company's direct investment overseas is that 'individuals differ only in character, not in ability'. Differences in human character stem not only from the environment in which people live; they also embody the variety of social, political, and economic systems of different countries as well as their historical and cultural setting. By understanding specific local differences through study and experience, Honda has been able to generalise its methods and philosophy so that they can take root anywhere in the world. The spread of Japanese TQC management and NH circle activities testifies to the universal relevance of Honda management and its regard for human resources.

Honda's global strategy entered a new phase after the first oil crisis in 1973, first in terms of direct investment overseas and then in the localisation of management. NH circles were set up in its overseas affiliates but the company did first take into account local characteristics as well as the special features of local political and economic systems.

Honda identified several characteristics that distinguish the West (the United States and Western Europe) from Japan, and these were potential hazards in the application of Japanese QC-circle activities in other countries. They come under three headings:

1 Contract-orientation

In a contract society, the duties of every white-collar, blue-collar and executive employee are specified. Employees are supposed to do no more than their assigned jobs. If they do, they run the risk of 'stealing' someone else's job. Even when there is some unexpected additional work, they may not see to it or not be allowed to see to it.

2 Stratification of Workers

In some countries, stratification based on religion or class is quite rigid, and devising new systems or innovative ways of doing things can then be difficult. Stratification cannot be ignored and is often embodied in the corporate hierarchy. Corporate stratification exists between white- and blue-collar workers, in the job hierarchy, and among persons of different academic background.

Among white-collar workers, top management is responsible for basic policies and is expected to assume vigorous leadership in implementing them. Those in mid-management and supervisory positions prepare specific plans and see that they are carried out. The staff is there to establish work standards, both 'hardware' and 'software'. Blue-collar workers – line workers and supervisors – are expected to work exactly as stipulated by the staff. Workers are not allowed to change the way work is done; only staff can propose changes in work procedures. The blue-collar worker is kept to one technical speciality or a very limited range of tasks. Workers wanting to master several skills may find the trade unions objecting. Skilled blue-collar workers in the West who may try to acquire new skills and know-how are apt to be secretive about their expertise.

3 Individual View of Work

The basic attitude towards work among Americans and Europeans is that work is a means to an end. They work to get a wage and are unwilling to sacrifice their personal lives for the sake of the job itself. The individual comes first, and individuals form horizontal bonds in the community. By contrast, Japanese society has a strong vertical orientation; individuals see themselves in terms of the group and do not wish to appear different from the others.

THE NH CIRCLE OUTSIDE JAPAN

Honda's experience in business abroad has enabled it to identify the obstacles to NH circle activities overseas. It overcame those obstacles, and NH circles (as well as QC circles) on the Japanese model are now to be found all over the world.

Quality control was first studied in the United States and started in Japan after World War II. The original techniques – known as statistical quality control (SQC) – are said to have been invented in 1926 by Walter A Shewhart of Bell Laboratories, an affiliate of the American Telephone and Telegraph Company. Under the enthusiastic guidance of Dr R Edwards Deming, they spread across the country. Adept at copying foreign techniques, the Japanese readily digested the principles of SQC and adopted them into an integrated, company-wide system of quality control that was even more effective than the original. In Japan they were extended to small-group activities of workers themselves – becoming a management technique and part of management philosophy. These activities and the concept of total quality control – the fruits of the special cultural and economic milieu of Japan – are in tune with basic human impulses and patterns of organisation.

1. QC activities provide incentive and fulfilment. Human beings everywhere share the same satisfaction from doing a job of work, making a product or providing a service, coming up with new and better products or ways of making them.
2. QC activities give one and all, regardless of social status or rank, the opportunity to show and develop their talents.
3. QC circles and TQC management encourage people to look at things from the point of view of others and to think and work together. This effect is an antidote to bureaucratisation.

In launching its NH circle activities worldwide, Honda stressed the following four points. First, incentive or motivation is vital. Japanese often feel more motivated by the reward of social recognition or honour – getting other people's confidence and regard – than by financial gain. In other countries, financial reward is usually the greatest incentive. Second, rewards should be clearly specified: who achieved what and how the achievement was rewarded. People like to have their achievements recognised. Third, people delight in festivals, and QC circle activities should be a release from day-to-day routine. Company-wide QC circle conventions are almost party occasions to which all can look forward. Fourth, the pursuit of efficiency through QC (NH) circle activities should not lead too easily to the transfer or dismissal of workers. A system that causes anxiety or distrust among workers can only end in failure. QC circle activities bear fruit only after a time and then perhaps only in bits and pieces.

MANAGEMENT AND QC CIRCLES

The car industry in Europe and the United States (especially GM, Ford, and other major car manufacturers) were startled by the rapid rise in the competitive strength of Japanese carmakers. They began to examine their business practices and concluded that the secret of their success lay principally in TQC management and QC circle activities. As for the small Japanese cars being economical and so easy to drive, they attributed this to the high quality of the many parts that went into the cars and their craftsmanlike assembly in keeping with Japanese tradition.

By now, TQC is so firmly established throughout Japanese industry that it is no longer a novelty: it is now part and parcel of normal management. It first appeared in the early 1960s as Japan entered the period of rapid economic growth, and became well established in the late 1960s and early 1970s during the heyday of Japan's rapid growth. The oil crisis of 1973 put TQC to a severe test. With the internationalisation of Japanese corporations in the mid- and late seventies, TQC came to be seen in Western economies as a unique Japanese management technique. Today, in the latter half of the 1980s, the strong competitiveness of Japanese corporations is the cause of trade frictions. The under-valuation of the yen has been corrected and the currency is much stronger. Japan's economy has to adjust itself to the international environment by restraining exports to a certain degree and promoting imports of foreign products. Meanwhile, TQC may have to be remodelled somewhat to the conditions of the post-industrial age.

TQC was adopted in all the major industries that took the lead in the post-war Japanese economy – first shipbuilding and steel and then the electrical and car industries. Each industry soon went beyond rudimentary QC on a factory basis to a company-wide management technique – total quality control to improve the quality of management through the participation of all employees. TQC and QC circle activities have proved effective in raising worker morale and bringing about qualitative improvements in management wherever they are practised anywhere in the world.

QC circles and TQC management are not fail-safe remedies for the shortcomings of management. Their effectiveness depends on whether the corporation has a management philosophy of its own and well thought out strategies for market competition. It depends on whether the company has developed a distinctive style and tradition of management. Nothing will work if the top management has no firm grasp of the situation in the industry nor any firm direction for their company. Vitality and direction, in turn, are only generated by a body that is heading somewhere, that has a vision of the future and knows how to get there.

Honda has distinctive systems of management and production, and so does Toyota with its 'just-in-time' production system. Only when a company has its own philosophy and the ability to create its own management and production systems can TQC and QC circle activities be used to strengthen those systems.

THE AMERICAN EXPERIENCE

Let us now look at the principles, policies and strategies of the Honda management system in building and operating its plants overseas, and at the way Honda management methods have made a name for themselves abroad. Honda's success in direct investment in the United States is a good illustration.

Honda of America was set up in the United States in 1959, the year the company first began to expand overseas. It concentrated on developing new motorcycle markets, and its efforts paid off handsomely. In 1979, when Honda opened its motorcycle factory in Ohio, it was the first Japanese manufacturer in the car industry to set up production on American soil. All others (including late comers such as Yamaha and Suzuki) had confined their efforts to exporting finished products to the United States. Nissan began producing trucks in Tennessee in 1983, and Toyota (in co-operation with GM) started turning out cars in California in 1984, both doing their best to localize management. By that time, Honda had already built a network of local parts makers and begun to manufacture car engines. It enjoyed the advantages of a front runner. Honda also benefitted from its early start in Canada where it built a car factory before any of its Japanese rivals.

Honda shifted first from the export of products to the export of capital, and then to a local work force and management. Kiyoshi Kawashima, who was president of Honda when the decision was made to build a factory in Ohio, claims that despite all the talk of 'Japanese management' and 'Japanese production systems', it is quite wrong to think of all Japanese companies and their management systems as one indistinguishable mass. Like every other Japanese corporation, Honda has its own distinctive history, traditions and corporate identity as well as a special management philosophy and strategy.

Honda management is not precisely the same in every country. As it is put into practice in Europe, the United States or South-east Asia, it is tailored to specific needs and conditions. There is nothing surprising about this, especially for Honda, where attention is customarily paid to 'individual differences'. Honda management is a mix of many elements drawn not only from Japanese experience but also from overseas experience, and this includes the response of users in the countries and local management know-how. Honda's production and management systems are a product of its global experience, including the valuable lessons learned in its initial project in the United States. Kawashima emphasises that all their endeavours are premised on the search for universal principles. They are ready, he says, to take on new challenges and gain new experience in the United States, aware of the need to keep their production and management systems abreast of the rapid changes taking place in the world.

Kawashima is firmly committed to the Honda motto 'Individuals differ only in character, not in ability'. Honda is not simply transplanting an a priori management system overseas for direct investment, hiring local workers, localizing management and so on. There is a lot of generalized and rather unreliable information about overseas production. Derogatory remarks about the quality of the American work force and charges that the unions in the United States tie management's hands are commonplace but should not be taken at face value. It is up to each corporation to find out for itself from its own experience what the situation really is. Kawashima calls Honda's venture in the United States a 'voyage of discovery' – exploring new terrain and finding out how to get along with the local people. Honda may even discover an America that has not yet been discovered by Americans.

The Ohio plant is separate from the Los Angeles-based American Honda Motor Company which is wholly funded by Honda Motors (capital of $200m in August 1986). Honda of America has capital of $478m (August 1986) and only 20 per cent of this comes from Honda Motors. The principles of Hondaism for the Ohio plant are taken partly from the parent company but some were worked out on-the-spot. Decisions made by the first and second presidents – Kazuo Nakagawa (now managing director of Honda Motors) and Shōichirō Irimajiri – in transplanting Hondaism to the United States illustrate their thinking about the goals of the company.

1. They sought to create a plant where workers co-operate with one another. Ways had to be found to discover and give full play to individual talents and encourage teamwork so that 'individual play' and teamwork complement each other.
2. At Honda of America, the words 'worker' and 'employee' have given way to the word 'associate'.

3. Honda of America has taken down the traditional barriers that separate offices (management and staff) from the factory floor. A company should be a place where everyone has easy access to different departments. When taking applications for factory employees, the company does not specify the nature of the openings; it simply announces that factory associates are needed because the company pursues a multi-skill training programme.

4. There is no labour union at Honda of America but this is not because the company's management is opposed to unions. Associates are free to organise a union if they wish. The management aims to provide humane conditions, to build an organisation that turns out high-quality products but also offers good human relationships. Its goal is to make the company so resilient that employees need not be laid off in the event of a recession.

5. Although American workers dislike uniforms, Honda of America decided to have the same white uniforms for its personnel as in its Japanese plants (with the name of the company and the wearer's nickname in red on the front). Everyone, from the new worker to the president, wears the same white uniform and everyone is on first-name terms. At meal times, management and associates use the same company dining hall. These practices are common to Honda group companies throughout the world.

In localising management, Honda continues to tackle new problems and issues. It faces the efforts of the United Auto Workers (UAW) in the United States to get Honda workers to join the union and their objection to company uniforms and even to the use of the term 'associates'. In its handling of matters such as these Honda secures a wider acceptance of Hondaism and all that it has come to mean.

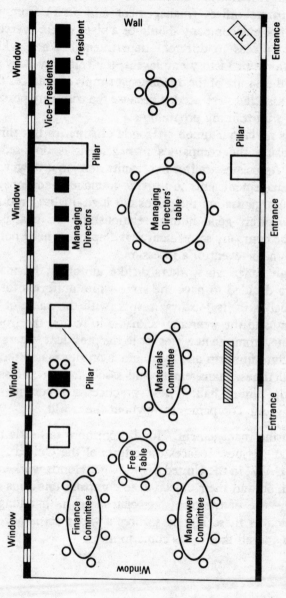

Figure 1 *Honda's joint boardroom* (see p. 33)

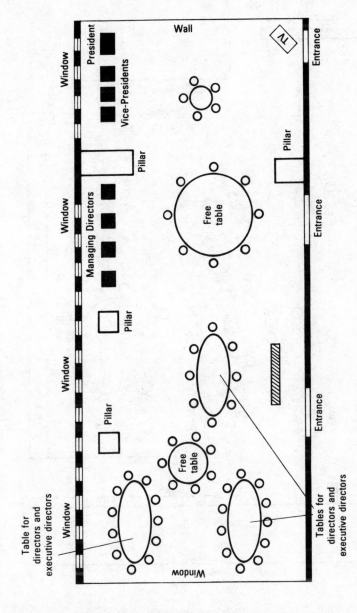

Figure 2 *Honda's joint boardroom* (see p. 33)

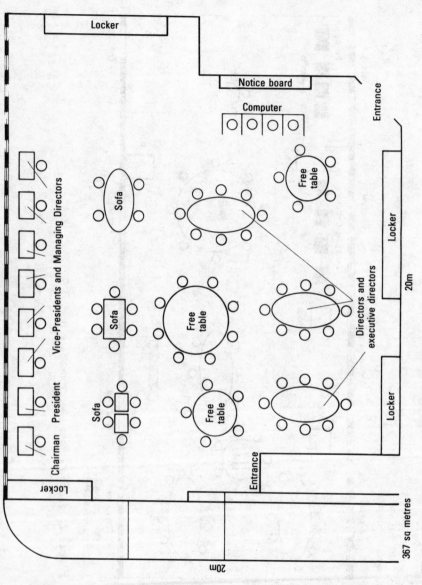

Figure 3 Honda's joint boardroom (see p. 33)

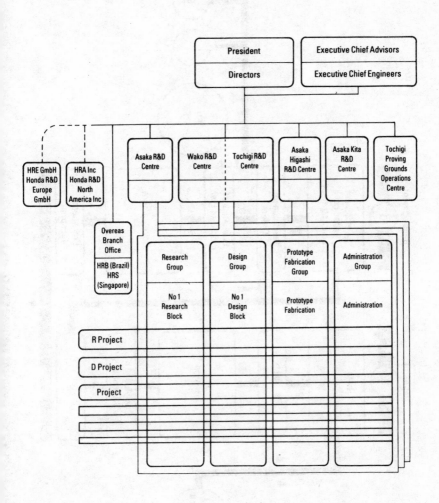

Figure 4 *The organisation and functions of Honda R&D* (see p. 64)

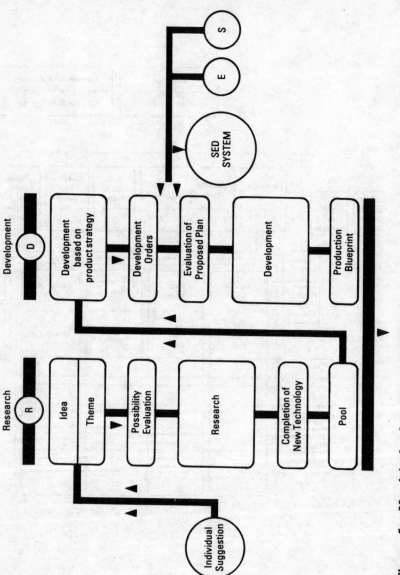

Figure 5 *Honda's development system* (see p. 64)

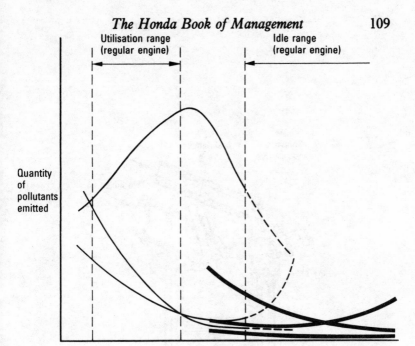

Utilisation range
(regular engine)

Idle range
(regular engine)

Quantity
of
pollutants
emitted

Dense ←   (air-fuel mixture)   → Thin

Regular Engine
Supply of a denser mixture of air and fuel decreases NOx but increases CO and HC.
Supply of a thinner mixture of air and fuel decreases CO and HC but increases NOx.
As the mixture grows thinner, NOx and CO will decrease but the engine may die.
Sources of Pollutants
The higher the temperature of the gas in the cylinder, the greater the amount of NOx emitted.
The more quickly the temperature of the gas in the cylinder falls in the process of expansion, the greater the amount of unignited fuel emitted as HC.
The greater the amount of dense fuel supplied, the greater the amount of CO emitted due to lack of oxygen resulting from oxidation.
Merits of CVCC Engine
Decrease in NOx by lowering the maximum combustion temperature.
Decrease in HC by prolonging the time the temperature of oxidation is maintained.
Decrease in CO by supplying very thin mixed gas so as to make sufficient oxygen available.

Figure 6 *Gas emission of regular engine and CVCC engine* (see p. 70)

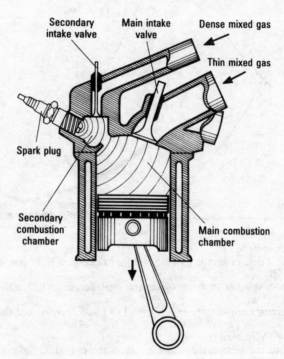

Figure 7 *The Civic Engine* (see p. 70)

Index